Spirit

THE BUDDHA

Geraldine Halls
Ashok Book Shop
Mysore
17.12.04

THE SERIES

The Spiritual Masters series is intended to serve as a first reader on the lives and teachings of some of the Masters who have enriched our life on this planet. They created a sublime body of knowledge, using such diverse means as song and silence to communicate their wisdom. They arose at different points in history, in diverse cultural and social contexts, yet they all spoke the language of love and compassion.

In today's troubled times, when people are getting increasingly divided along religious lines, the message of these Teachers assumes greater relevance. This series attempts to reach out to the modern reader by presenting the Master and his teaching in a simple, narrative format.

The Buddha and Sai Baba are the first two titles in this series. Subsequent titles would include Sant Dhyaneshwar, Adi Sankara, Mahavira, Jesus, Zarathustra, Kabir, Meerabai, Guru Nanak and Khwaja Moinuddin Chishti.

Other titles in this series:

Sai Baba *Sonavi Desai*

Spiritual Masters

THE BUDDHA

Supriya Rai

Indus Source Books

Smriti Books

Co-Published by:

INDUS SOURCE BOOKS
203, Banaji House
361, Dr. D.N. Road
Fort, Mumbai-400 001
(INDIA)

SMRITI BOOKS
124, Siddarth Enclave
New Delhi-110 014
(INDIA)

ISBN: 81-87967-63-3

Distributors:
NEW AGE BOOKS
A-44 Naraina Phase-I
New Delhi-110 028 (INDIA)
Email: nab@vsnl.in
Website: www.newagebooksindia.com

Printed at Shri Jainendra Press
A-45 Naraina Phase-I
New Delhi-110 028 (INDIA)

*An offering of love and gratitude
to Guruji
Sri Sri Ravishankar*

ACKNOWLEDGEMENTS

I would like to express my sincere gratitude to Dr. Kalpakam Shankarnarayanan, Director at the K. J. Somaiya Centre for Buddhist Studies, Mumbai, for her quiet reassurance and support, without which this book would not have been possible.

My thanks are also due to:

Robert Lewis Hoover, who so generously permitted the use of his painting for the front cover.

Dickie Khambatta, for unravelling the mysteries of paper and printing technologies, encouraging us to self-publish.

Gouri Dange, our editor, whose probing questions helped clarify my own thoughts.

Sonavi Desai, my partner, who shares my dreams and anguish, for Indus Source and for life in general.

Meenakshi Lath and Dr. Vidya Vencatesan, who read the early drafts and spoke many kind words of encouragement.

And to Amma, for slaying the dragons.

Most of all, I would like to thank my husband Vijay and my son, Nandan, for the abundance of their love and understanding.

NOTE TO THE READER

Many consider the Buddha, Siddhartha Gautama, to be one of the greatest humans ever to walk this planet. As Sir Edwin Arnold wrote in the preface to his epic poem *Light of Asia*, "no single act or word ...mars the perfect purity and tenderness of this Indian teacher, who united the truest princely qualities with the intellect of a sage and the passionate devotion of a martyr."

There is considerable debate about the exact year of the Buddha's birth. The most widely accepted date is based on the Sri Lankan chronicles Dipavamsa and Mahavamsa. According to these sources, the Buddha was born in 563 BC and he passed into nirvana in the year 483 BC. Given to contemplation from an early age, he left home at 29 to seek a solution to the problem of human suffering. He attained enlightenment at 35 and spent the next 45 years of his life travelling along the public road that existed then – the Northern Route (Uttarapatha), preaching his doctrine of Liberation. The Northern Route started in Savatthi, turning east towards Kapilavatthu, then south to Kusinara and Vesali, before crossing the Ganges to enter Magadha.

The Buddha's teachings spread far, even in his own lifetime. Today, Buddhism is a vibrantly alive religion, widely practised in the East, in a plethora of sects and traditions that would perhaps confound him, should he ever return. The last century saw Buddhism spread to Western countries – the universality of the Buddha's message, the absence of dogma in his teachings and his assertion that he was only what other men might also become, all served to attract many followers.

This narration attempts to bring the Buddha alive for a contemporary audience, by interweaving actual events from his life with fictional encounters. Magadha and Kosala, two of the many kingdoms that extended royal patronage to the Buddha, form the backdrop to this tale. Three narrators take the reader through the Buddha's life. Two of them existed, we know for sure – they are Rahula, the son of Buddha; and Ananda, Buddha's cousin, who became his disciple and later, his personal attendant. The third narrator is a creature of fiction – Triguna, King Bimbisara's charioteer.

Buddhist folklore mentions Rahula almost in passing. Accounts of his first meeting with his father, his entry into the Sangha, and some anecdotes about the Buddha personally correcting young Rahula's behaviour are all that can be found. None of these suggest that Rahula was accorded a unique status, for the Buddha would have done as much for any young novice. Buddhist records depict Rahula as a devoted yet restrained son of an exalted father.

The Rahula of this book transgresses Buddhist tradition by freely expressing the yearning that a child feels for his father. This transgression derives sanction from the universal nature of human experience. Rahula was a very young boy when he was ordained. And young boys have not changed much over the millennia – Rahula played pranks then, as boys do now. What made Rahula's life unusual was his early entry into monastic life and the awe-inspiring personality of his father. Surely there must have been times when he yearned for a parent in the Buddha. What was it like for a young boy to grow up in the company of monks who meditated all day and ate sparingly? What became of Rahula's boyhood? Through this characterization of Rahula, we explore what it must have been like to have the Buddha as a father.

Triguna, the charioteer, serves as the *sutradhar* for the period involving King Bimbisara of Magadha and King Pasenadi of Kosala. These two men were related by marriage and were great supporters of the Sangha. Triguna takes the reader through the early years of the Sangha and gives a glimpse of the political climate in which Buddhism developed. The Sangha faced external difficulties and problems from within, yet the Way of the Master remained ever compassionate. His teachings fuelled a transformation even in the lives of ordinary folk, which is reflected in the character of Triguna as he progresses with his narration.

Triguna is an observer, participating on the fringes of King Bimbisara's relationship with the Buddha. Traditionally, charioteers were trusted lieutenants of the King – they performed a sensitive job and required the equivalent of today's high security clearances. That enabled them to be privy to some of the King's more personal moments. Triguna, by outliving the King, is also able to carry that particular narrative a little further into the Buddha's own lifetime.

The other narrator, Ananda, served as a keeper of records during the Buddha's lifetime. He accompanied him everywhere and as a result, heard all his discourses. He was reportedly endowed with a phenomenal memory and could repeat these discourses verbatim. His gentle and sympathetic disposition, however, caused him great difficulty in breaking through the attachments of this world into the light of the Buddha's knowledge. His narration here echoes the devoted yet somewhat bumbling manner in which he led his life as the Buddha's attendant.

The attempt in this book is to present the Buddha as a human being, although he has been deified now and a formal religion built around his teachings. The period in Indian history in which the Buddha lived and taught was one of intellectual ferment; many philosophers and religious leaders questioned Brahminism and established beliefs. What differentiated the Buddha and his teachings was his emphasis on direct experience, without reliance on anyone else – be it teacher or superior being – for the ultimate deliverance.

Many liberties have been taken in this book – some with chronology, some with tone, some with presentation of the Master himself. I seek the indulgence of Buddhist Masters, those who are present now, those who have gone before and those yet to come.

CONTENTS

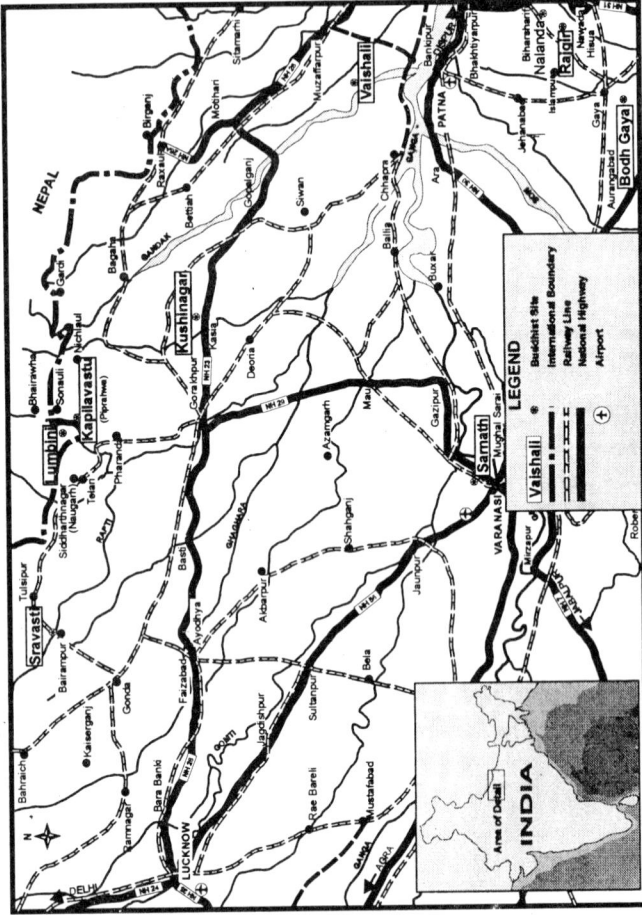

Map of the region in which the Buddha travelled and taught.

Book I: Rahula
Son of Buddha

SHRAVANA

The Dhamma talk had just been concluded. We sat for a while in the enveloping silence, profoundly moved by the wisdom that had been revealed. Gradually, the lay disciples began to disperse and the *bhikkhus* moved back to their dwellings. I, too, gathered up the folds of my robe and walked down the pathway to my hut.

It was during evening meditation that I sensed his presence. I opened my eyes to find a little brown face with bright, curious eyes peering at me from behind the doorway. As I nodded, he stepped in, his face crinkled into an impish smile. He was a scruffy young lad of about ten. A coarse thatch of hair, splayed, calloused feet, a bony frame – yet he shone with keen intelligence.

"I am Shravana," he said, bowing tentatively. "I have walked with you now for more than two days, Sire! Thank God we have stopped here, for I was getting really tired!"

"What are you doing here? Won't your parents miss you?" I asked with some concern.

"I have no family really – a distant uncle gives me shelter, in exchange for long hours of toil in the fields. I saw you walking through the forest on your way to the monastery here and I followed you. I have never seen people treat others the way

3

you monks do. I want to be like you! Please can I become a monk, sir?"

I gazed deep into those eager brown eyes, listening to echoes from my own childhood. This was I, about 30 years ago, when I first met Father! I had experienced the same wonder and awe when I had seen the monks of the Sangha. They radiated wisdom and compassion that had stirred the depths of my little heart.

I sent Shravana off to wash first and asked one of the younger monks to see if we had any food for the lad. I also summoned a couple of the senior monks, to consult with them on this new addition to our group. News of his arrival spread and the *bhikkhus* gathered, his chirping voice drawing smiles and kindly nods. They fed him some sesame rice and he was delighted. He returned to my hut soon enough and, squatting comfortably by my side, he began pleading again...

"Please, kind sir, I want to be like you! Please, tell me who you are!"

"I am Rahula, son of Buddha," I heard myself say.

I was as startled as Shravana by my disclosure. I had been a monk for 30 years now, and never had I introduced myself like this. For I was raised as one of many, never as a special one. When I joined the Sangha, my young heart had celebrated the ecstasy of being with Father, but in truth, I was raised by his great disciple, the Venerable Sariputta. And yet, it was Father's voice that coursed through my veins, his compassion and understanding nourishing my little being as it struggled with the rigours of a monk's life. Everyday, I bowed in all the directions he ruled with his insight and knowledge. I had lived every moment in his shadow, grateful for the tranquillity it offered. In a hundred different ways, I *was* the son of Buddha!

"I have heard about the Buddha. Are you really his son, O Venerable Monk? What was it like, to be his son?" Shravana asked in hushed tones, his innocence permitting him the freedom of candour. The *bhikkhus* had wondered too, but had never dared to ask.

"I was born the son of Buddha but I am a *bhikkhu* now, like all my companions. We travel together and spread his teaching for the benefit of all beings," I replied.

But Shravana was undeterred.

"When did you become a monk? What did you do when you were a young boy? Did you get to play in the forest all day long?" he asked, wide-eyed at the possibilities.

His questions began to bring back old memories and I closed my eyes to see them better...

A little boy was kneeling on the forest floor, sharp pebbles bruising his skin. Solemn young men with shorn heads stood by silently. His heart threatened to break out of his rib cage as a monk sharpened a fearsome razor on a flat stone. Then he glanced at his father and his fears fell away. Moments later, his lustrous locks lay strewn among the pebbles and dried leaves, and he knew his life had changed forever.

"I was ordained when I was seven years old. That's when I first met Father, when he returned to visit us at the Palace in Kapilavatthu," I said.

Shravana's eyes opened large and round, "A palace?"

"Yes, a palace!" I said, amused at the boy's wonder. "I was born Prince Rahula, son of Crown Prince Siddhartha, heir to the Sakya throne! That's right, the Buddha was born in a royal household. My grandfather, King Shuddhodana, ruled over the Sakya kingdom at the foothills of the great Himalayas."

"Why did the Buddha leave the Palace and become a wandering teacher? I would never, ever leave a palace for the creatures of the forest!" Shravana exclaimed and the *bhikkhus* laughed out loud.

"It's a long story and you should rest now," I said. But the lad shook his head vigorously, pleading to know more about Father, about my youth and about my life as his son.

"Very well then," I said, giving in.

The *bhikkhus* were amazed at what this lad had achieved. It was not often that they heard tales about the Buddha and his family. The hushed reminiscences of the older *bhikkhus* – Father's companions and cousins who had joined the Sangha – were their only sources of information. Father himself never spoke of the past. As the *bhikkhus* settled down on makeshift cushions of folded robes, their faces mirrored the eager anticipation of the young lad.

As I travelled back in time to my childhood, the fragrance of Mother's perfume returned to haunt me. Even early in the morning, as I buried my head in her lap for a few extra moments of sleep, she would smell of that wonderful soft fragrance. To my adoring eyes, she seemed bathed in moonbeams and frangipani.

I inhaled deeply and started my tale:

"My earliest memories are of the boundless love and caring attention of my mother and my grandparents. They watched indulgently as my friends and I played in the Palace gardens and splashed around in the shallow pond by the apple orchard. On special occasions, Mother would dress me up in fine silk, embellished with gold thread, and I wore strings of pearls and gemstones around my neck. A kindly old tutor would try to make me sit still for a few hours every morning, to learn music, mathematics and poetry. He told me Father played such an exquisite flute that the birds stopped to listen.

I was very small when Father left home, just a baby. Mother often told me, 'Rahula, your father is a special man, on a special mission. When he finds what he is seeking, his teachings will bring great comfort to all beings. Yours will be a unique inheritance.' I did not understand much of that. But I loved the stories she told me about him.

Father's birth had been foretold. One night, his mother, Queen Mahamaya, dreamed that an enormous white elephant with six tusks had descended from heaven to the sound of celestial music. She was overcome with fear, till she saw that he held a bright pink lotus in his trunk, which he placed in her womb. She awoke in a state of bliss, with that heavenly music still ringing in her ears. Grandfather was very excited too, when she told him about her dream. He called upon the astrologers and religious leaders of his kingdom to reveal its secret. They said the dream was a message from the heavens that a unique and gifted child would soon be born to the Queen. There was great rejoicing in the Palace and soon enough, Queen Mahamaya was expecting a child.

The story of Father's birth and of the early years of his youth has become something of a legend in Kapilavatthu. If you like, I can narrate it to you but after that, you must be off for the night."

"Oh *yes!*" exclaimed Shravana, clapping his hands in delight.

The Tale of Prince Siddhartha

Lumbini was a magical grove. Graceful ferns sprayed out of rocky nooks, joyously wafting the fragrance of the moist, fertile earth up to the high reaches of the Sal trees that grew there. Flowers ran amok in the grove. Rhododendrons bloomed like splashes of sindoor and the majestic spreading branches of Mandara trees were aflame with blossoms. Lantanas jostled gleefully with bluebells and wild daisies carpeted the forest floor. Birdcalls rang through the air as the feathered creatures went about their mysterious business. Butterflies floated by, weaving dreams of light and play – there was ecstasy at being alive in Lumbini.

Nothing was insignificant here, no creature too small or ordinary. Each leaf, each blushing petal, each golden drop of sunlight that filtered through the branches was a chosen one. Chosen to witness a great event that was to occur in the grove. For you see, it was here that the little Prince Siddhartha was born.

Queen Mahamaya was on her way to Ramagama, the capital of Koliya. She was heavy with child and was on her way to her parents' home, as was the custom. The forest enchanted her and she stopped awhile. As she walked towards an Ashoka tree, she suddenly felt uneasy and grabbed a branch to steady herself. Standing there, in the early morning light, she gave birth to a little boy. Her attendants washed him and wrapped him in soft robes, remarking on his great beauty.

The little one was named Siddhartha, meaning 'one who has realized his quest.' King Shuddhodana was delighted that he now had an heir and his people celebrated with him. He invited saints and astrologers to bless his son and decipher what the stars foretold for the little Prince. They examined the peculiar markings on the boy's feet, pored over the charts and declared he would be an 'Emperor of All Directions', unparalleled in history. And King Shuddhodana's eyes brimmed over with pride and joy.

A hermit sage, Master Asita Kaladevela, lived in the hills outside the capital. On hearing about the Prince, he trudged down to the Palace to see him. Master Asita was revered throughout the kingdom and King Shuddhodana personally welcomed the great teacher. Strangely though, upon seeing the little Prince, the sage burst into tears and was inconsolable.

The King became anxious. He asked, with great concern, "Is something amiss, Master? Will some terrible misfortune befall my child?"

"Oh no, no!" cried Master Asita. "This child will become a great Master one day. He will realize great truths and his legacy will endure for centuries to come. It is I who is stricken by misfortune , Your Majesty! I weep because I will not live long enough to hear him speak." And he went away, unable to contain his grief.

The King was alarmed at this prophecy. He wanted his son to rule after him, not renounce the world to become a monk. He made up his mind to fill his son's life with all the joys and treasures of this world. He would make sure Siddhartha never felt the need to visit hermits or sages.

Within a week of Siddhartha's birth, Queen Mahamaya passed away. Later, the King married her sister, Mahapajapati, fondly known as Gotami. She tended to little Siddhartha's needs as if he were her own.

Siddhartha's childhood companions were his cousins, Devadatta and Ananda, Mahanama and Aniruddha, Bhaddiya and Kimbila. Another dear friend wasKaludayi, who was the son of a palace official. But Siddhartha would often slip away from the group to sit by himself, lost in a world of silent contemplation. "Siddhartha is a dreamer, perhaps he will be a poet!" they said.

Once, when he was nine years old, Siddhartha was strolling in the wooded gardens of the Palace. Suddenly, he heard cries of such anguish that he could not tell if they came from a man or a beast. There was a horrible thud and he saw a swan lying wounded on the ground, stunned by its fall. Siddhartha rushed towards it and gently pulled an arrow out of its side. Pressing the wound to stem the bleeding, he carried it inside. A maid was sent to make a poultice of medicinal herbs, while young Siddhartha wrapped his own jacket around the frightened, shivering creature.

Just then, Devadatta rushed in. "Have you seen the swan I shot down?" he asked.

Siddhartha pointed silently to the bird on the rug. Devadatta rushed to claim it but Siddhartha stepped forward to stop him. A serious argument ensued.

"The swan is mine, Siddhartha. I shot it down."
"You may have. But I saved it, so it is mine now."
" It was flying in the sky – it did not belong to anyone then. I brought it down, it is rightfully mine!"
"I am protecting it," said Siddhartha stubbornly. "It is mine!"

Devadatta tried to grab the bird but Siddhartha pushed him away firmly. They could not resolve their dispute and decided to place the matter before the King's Council. The men pondered and debated the issue, with many supporting Devadatta's claim, for a hunter always staked the first claim to his prey. But then an old councillor declared firmly,

"A life belongs to him who tries to save it, who cares for it. A life cannot belong to one who is only trying to destroy it. Let the swan be given to Siddhartha."

11

The entire Council agreed with these wise words. Devadatta was furious, but he had to give in. Siddhartha cared for the bird and when its wounds had healed, he carried it to the forest and set it free.

Young Siddhartha was a serious student and soon became adept at archery, literature and music. As he grew older, he was initiated into philosophy and the study of ancient texts. He had an inquisitive mind and would question his teachers, often to a point where they could not resolve his dilemmas. Young Devadatta was keen to surpass Siddhartha, but he never managed to defeat him – neither in debate nor in sport.

Siddhartha's universe was defined by palace walls. The King had built three wonderful palaces for his son. One was made of wood and lined with sweet cedar, to keep him warm in the winter months. Another was built of marble, its cool floor and pillared verandahs designed to keep the Prince comfortable in the hot summer months. The third palace was built of bricks, with a beautiful, blue-tiled roof, to shield the young Prince from the rains that pelted the region during the monsoons.

The palaces were surrounded by sculpted gardens with tinkling fountains, flowering trees and lotus ponds, so that everywhere the Prince looked, he would see blossoming beauty and bounteous joy – the King was doing his best to ensure that Siddhartha found everything he sought within Palace bounds.

But the King could see his son was given to long periods of meditative silence. And then he would recall Master Asita's prophecy and the fear of Siddhartha leaving home would grip his heart.

"How do I ensure Siddhartha becomes the next King and not a monk?" he asked his ministers. They recommended that a suitable bride be found for him, for once he became a family man, his ties with the Palace would be too strong for him to embark on a monk's life.

And so it came to pass that Mother Gotami arranged for all the fair maidens in the Kingdom to meet the Prince and receive gifts from him. He stood by a podium on which many pieces of jewellery had been arranged on silver trays. The young ladies walked up shyly and the ministers watched keenly, to see if Siddhartha liked any of them. But their Prince politely handed out the jewels, unmoved by their beauty.

The last maiden had received her present and the ministers sat crestfallen, sighing in disappointment. Just then, a magnificent young lady appeared. The lustre of her youth was enhanced by the sweetness of her demeanour. She walked gracefully up to the Prince and smiled, asking, "Is there no gift for me then, Your Highness?"

Young Siddhartha was startled and a little confused. Then, with a sparkle in his eye, he took off his jewelled necklace and tied it to her waist.

The ministers were overjoyed. The girl was Princess Yashodhara, daughter of King Suppabuddha. She was, in fact, a cousin of their young Prince. King Shuddhodana formally asked for her hand in marriage to his son. But King

13

Suppabuddha demanded a display of the Prince's prowess in the martial arts before giving away his daughter. For Siddhartha was known to be contemplative and soft-hearted.

A contest was arranged in a large open ground in the city. Siddhartha was a quiet lad but his concentration was intense, his abilities formidable. He sent his arrow further than the best archer in the kingdom could. With his sword, he slit a great tree in half so neatly that for a few moments it stood balanced on the lower part, until a gust of wind blew it down. And when it came to riding, he left his competitors far behind as he rode his horse, Kanthaka, at great speed.

His victory led to disgruntled whispers among the other contestants. Anyone can win with a horse as fast as Kanthaka, they said. And so Siddhartha was challenged to ride a black stallion, a bad tempered beast that had never allowed any man to sit astride him. Only one of the challengers, Arjuna, managed to ride him once around the stadium. But then the beast turned his huge head, grabbed Arjuna's feet with his teeth and pulled him off. Arjuna would have been trampled to death if attendants and armed guards had not rushed in.

A murmur of agitation went through the spectators – would Siddhartha be able to subdue this beast? All eyes were on the Prince as he calmly approached the stallion, spoke a few soft words in his ears and mounted him. To the utter amazement of the crowd, the huge beast proceeded to take Siddhartha docilely around the field, without a trace of bad temper in his gait! The crowds were ecstatic and cheered their Prince. King Suppabuddha graciously congratulated him, proud to have his daughter wed such a fine young man.

The marriage of Siddhartha and Yashodhara was celebrated with great festivity in Kapilavatthu. King Shuddhodana was now at peace. He was sure his son would succeed him to the throne. He still would not permit him to leave the Palace grounds, however, and made sure that only young and healthy attendants waited on the young couple.

"Let no sick or old person dwell near my son," he ordered. "He must see joy, youth and good health around him, always!" If ever an attendant took ill, he was quickly removed from service and not permitted to return until he had fully recovered. Musicians and dancers entertained the newlyweds. A huge wall shielded the young couple from the world that lay beyond. Everywhere they gazed, there was enchantment and luxury.

But the young Prince's heart was restless and unknown longings stirred within him. He wanted to know how people who were not princes and noblemen lived; what life was like beyond the Palace walls. He asked his father many times for permission to go out into the city. King Shuddhodana made up new festivals and celebrations to distract Siddhartha.

Finally, though, he could refuse his son no more. So he arranged for the whole city to be bedecked, as if for a festival. The houses were whitewashed, streets were swept and trees festooned with cloth buntings. Garlands of flowers were strung outside all homes. The sick and the elderly were asked to stay indoors. People were also asked to put off carrying their dead through the streets until the Prince's visit was over. Only when these arrangements were in place was the Prince was allowed out, with his attendant, Channa.

15

As Siddhartha emerged from the Palace gates, the people of the kingdom cheered him and showered him with petals and perfumed water. He rode through the streets, taking in the sights and sounds, wide-eyed, like a child at a fair. He saw how happy everyone looked and how energetic the people of the kingdom were. They had nice houses and wore gaily-coloured clothes. Children too were well-nourished and had bright, cheerful faces.

Just as the tour was about to end, however, an old beggar emerged from a decrepit hut. His bent body was weakened by age and ill-health. His hair was sparse and grey, his eyes had sunk deep into his head. His clothes in tatters, his teeth missing and with a foul odour emanating from his unwashed body, he begged the people in the street to give him something to eat.

Siddhartha stopped his carriage, perplexed at this sight. "Why is that man so bent and shrivelled, Channa? Can he not walk upright? And why is his hair not black and shiny, like ours? What has happened to his teeth?"

"He is an old man, my Prince," replied the attendant.

"Old? What is that? Was he born like that?"

"No, no, Your Highness! When a person lives long, that is what happens. They grow old, the body becomes weak and wrinkled, teeth fall out," Channa explained.

"What a terrible thing this is, Channa! Does it happen to everyone? Even to princes? Will it happen to me? To Father,

16

Mother, even Yashodhara?"cried Siddhartha, staring at the beggar in horror.

"Yes, Your Highness! If we live long enough, this is what will happen to all of us. Old age tarnishes this body and it is something no one can stop," said Channa, as he gently led the Prince away.

Siddhartha was shocked and disturbed. They rode back to the Palace in silence. A few days later, he asked to be allowed another visit to the city, but without any of the earlier arrangements this time. The King knew that the young Prince would not be at peace until he saw more of the world outside. Channa accompanied the Prince on this visit too. They both stepped out in ordinary clothes, to be able to mingle better with the citizens.

The Prince saw the people go about their daily chores – the blacksmith hammered away at the anvil, the fisherman bargained lustily for a better price, the cloth merchant tried to persuade young women to buy his brightly coloured saris, children played in courtyards...everything seemed to be working to some secret, happy rhythm. Channa heaved a sigh of relief – perhaps this visit would be uneventful. But it was not to be.

As they walked down the main street, Siddhartha heard a man crying in pain. He rushed into a nearby lane to find a man writhing in agony on the road. He was foaming at the mouth, gasping for breath. Siddhartha knelt by his side and tried to ease his suffering by stroking his brow, telling him to calm down, but it did not help at all.

17

"Channa, what is the matter with him? Why is he frothing and gasping? Why can't I make this strange thing go away?"

Channa tried to drag the Prince away, saying, "He has the plague, Your Highness! You should not go near him, you may catch it too!"

"Catch what? What is this plague?" cried the young Prince.

"It is a sickness, my Prince. It afflicts people and makes them very ill. Their blood gets poisoned and it makes them gasp for air. It is an extremely painful condition."

"Why did it strike him? Could he not see it coming and run away? Please do something about it, Channa!" asked Siddhartha, agitated now.

"Sickness is an unseen, unknown enemy that strikes at will, my Prince. There is nothing anyone can do about it. Once afflicted, people just suffer until they finally die."

"Die?! And what is that?" asked Siddhartha, startled that there were so many painful conditions in this world that he was unaware of. Silently, Channa pointed to a funeral procession passing by.

Siddhartha watched as a group of grieving men walked past, carrying a sleeping man on a wooden palette. He was all shrivelled up, like an old guava. His mouth lay open in a frozen grimace and he didn't seem to mind the bumpy ride, as the palette-bearers stumbled along on the road leading to the river bank. Then, as Siddhartha watched in horror, they placed the sleeping man on a pile of logs and set it all on fire. He could not bear the sight and cried out in fear,

"Channa, hurry! We must stop them! Why are they burning that poor man? Why doesn't he get up and run away from the flames?"

"He feels nothing, Your Highness! The body you see is just a shell that housed the man he was before. He breathes no more, he is dead."

Siddhartha gazed at the burning pyre in horror. "Dead? He will just burn away and become ashes? Can no one stop this terrible thing? Will I die too? And you? And Father, Mother? Yashodhara too?"

"That is the one thing that will surely happen to each one of us, my Lord! There is no being who can escape death," replied Channa, watching with a heavy heart as the young Prince tried to cope with what he had seen that day.

Siddhartha spent the next few days deep in thought. Old age, sickness and death – what terrible things these were. There had to be relief from this suffering, he thought, there must be some way.

He now began to ride out more often into the city. Once he saw a man in orange robes, glowing with tranquillity, begging quietly for his meal. Channa told him this man was a monk – he had given up all the worldly pleasures to seek eternal bliss. Siddhartha was struck by his peaceful appearance and resolved that he, too, would become a monk.

19

As he observed the life of ordinary citizens, restlessness began to gnaw at Siddhartha's heart. He saw many people in a state of poverty, illness and ignorance. They lived lives of cringing misery, with no means to fight hunger or disease. They just stumbled from one day to the next, resigned to their fate.

Siddhartha also realised that high caste priests were the only ones permitted to recite prayers and perform rituals to appease the various deities that influenced human life. He wondered why this was so – if no one was spared the tragedies of old age, sickness and death, why were some people permitted higher knowledge and others not? Questions plagued him and he walked about restlessly in the gardens.

"Even my Father, who is King, has to depend on the priest to chant the verses at a religious ceremony," he thought.

It distressed him that the poor were compelled to appease the priests, especially for rituals related to birth, death and marriage. How could such rituals help the family, which was sunk into penury? The chanting of sacred texts did not help them lead better lives, he observed. If the solution to human suffering lay in the power of sacred words – why, then, did so many continue to suffer? Where lay true deliverance?

Increasingly, he began to believe that it lay in individual effort towards release from suffering, from the unending cycles of birth and death. He was convinced there was a way and he was determined to find it.

It was late now and Shravana lay slumped with exhaustion. But he sat up the moment I stopped narrating my story.

"My mind is awake though my body is sleeping!" he declared, to the great merriment of the monks. "Please can you continue, Venerable Rahula, only for a bit?"

I had long surrendered to the lad's innocence...

"Mother knew that Father's desire to find a solution to the problems of human suffering would lead him away from us. She never once dissuaded him, though. Not even when I was born. He named me 'Rahula', meaning 'fetter' or 'tie' – I guess he felt I was one more bond that would restrain him from leaving home in search of the Way.

Father asked for permission to leave the Palace and study with the renowned masters who lived in the neighbouring kingdoms of Magadha and Kosala. Grandfather knew then that there was little he could do to stop the prophecy of Master Asita from coming true. But he decided to make one last attempt. He asked Udayin, one of Father's friends, to arrange a party for the Prince. The finest musicians and dancers were summoned and the Palace gardens were festooned with colourful lanterns. It was a full-moon night and the gardens looked enchanting.

After the guests had departed, Father sat and gazed at the moonlit sky for a long time. He decided to leave that very night. He asked Channa to harness his horse and he left, with one last look at his sleeping wife and baby. That baby was me, of course."

21

I gazed at young Shravana for a long, silent moment. He was pure and tender, like a lotus bud. He too would blossom in the Sangha one day.

"We can meet again tomorrow and I will continue the story," I said to him. "We must find your uncle, too. He must be worried about you."

Shravana appeared to think that was extremely unlikely but he agreed to go back to town with a *bhikkhu* to seek his uncle's permission before joining the order. "Can we go to my village after you have finished the tale?" he asked earnestly. "Oh please, can I stay here for a few days before we go back to Uncle?"

He was obviously worried he would not be permitted to join us. But we had to observe the rules of the Sangha. And, what's more, this rule had been laid down when Grandfather had complained bitterly at my ordainment! I smiled as I recalled that day – the Teacher of the Great Way to Liberation, the Venerable Gautama Buddha, had actually been scolded by his father! Since then, we did not initiate young boys into the order unless we had the explicit permission of their elders.

I observed how courteously Shravana bowed when he took leave of the *bhikkhus* for the night. And how eager the monks were to take care of him – one offered him a spare robe as a warm shawl for the night, another promised to bring some extra food offering for him the next day. They patted his head kindly and enjoyed his non-stop chatter. The arrival of a young one is always a joyous event in nature, I thought, as I watched them wend their way to their huts.

We continued the tale of Father's youth the next day, after the midday meal. Shravana had woken up early that morning, with the *bhikkhus*. He had washed in the cold stream and had spent the morning cleaning their huts. He had already made himself at home, I observed. He ate with the younger monks, watching their silent, mindful manner and emulating it. Then we all sat under the shade of a rain tree and they waited for me to continue the previous day's tale.

My thoughts turned to Mother again, that ever loving, gentle soul, with molten brown eyes that seemed to carry a secret through the eons. I told them of my youth…

"I knew that both Mother and my grandmother, Gotami, were very proud of Father. My grandfather, King Shuddhodana would always be overcome with emotion, though, and would walk away when Father's name was mentioned. So I gathered that he missed him terribly. All in all, I knew that my father was a unique man, different from all others – but I missed him too.

When Channa, Father's attendant, played with his son, I watched with an strange sadness filling my heart. Would Father have tossed me in the air like that too? Sometimes Mother took me with her to the villages where she tended to the sick and the poor. There, I watched little children run up to their fathers as they returned home from the fields, leaping into their arms in delight. They would squeal and squirm when their fathers' stubble grazed their skin.

I had never felt a father's rough chin on my cheeks. I knew not what it was to sit at a father's knee and watch him fix the

23

broken wheel of a toy chariot, nor to have him explain the
heavenly spectacle of the night skies. I longed to discover a
gift on my pillow that my father had brought back, from a
tour to magical, distant lands. I missed my father as much as
Grandpa did. Only, I hadn't even seen him."

I sat quietly for a while, observing my breath, as I relived the
pangs of little Rahula. He had been unable to comprehend
why his Father never visited, why his Mother had given up
wearing jewellery and adorning herself, like other mothers
did. She had refused all comforts of the Palace and lived in
simple robes, eating frugal meals. She said she could not bear
to live a life of luxury when her husband was begging for his
meals and living in a forest.

And yet again, I heard Father's voice, speaking in calm,
measured tones:

*All things that are born must pass. Impermanence is the
nature of all phenomena. When you dwell in mindfulness,
you will gain true Understanding of the nature of our
existence.*

My reverie was broken as Shravana piped up, "What
happened next, Venerable Rahula?"

"Well, one fine day, after seven years, Father appeared.
Rather, Kaludayi appeared first, shocking everyone with his
bhikkhu's robes.

You see, after Father left, his friend Kaludayi had become
one of Grandpa's trusted advisors. The news of Father's

attaining Enlightenment had reached us in Kapilavatthu and also that he was teaching in Magadha, at the Bamboo Forest. So Grandpa sent Kaludayi and Channa to Magadha, to get us news of him.

They had been away a long time. Just as everyone was wondering what could have happened to them, Kaludayi appeared with the news that Father had indeed found the way to end human suffering. He said Father was now known as the Buddha, the Enlightened One, and he would be visiting us soon, perhaps in the next month itself!

Kaludayi had been so deeply moved by the Buddha's compassion and the infinite beauty of his teachings that he had asked to be ordained as a monk. Poor Channa too had wanted to become a monk, but he felt constrained by his responsibilities at the Palace.

What tremendous excitement there was at the news that Kaludayi brought! Grandpa could hardly contain himself. He shouted excitedly at everyone.

'I want the whole city washed and perfumed! Line the avenues he will walk with garlands of the most fragrant flowers! Shower him with petals and rose water as he walks and let not his feet be soiled! Music, there must be music in the city!! My son is coming home!!'

He personally supervised all the arrangements and harassed Grandma with his incessant questions about the meals she planned to serve when their son came home again. He wanted to plan each detail himself!

'Make sure they are vegetarian meals. Arrange for the choicest fruits and nuts to be brought in from all corners of our kingdom. Make sure there are plenty of sweets – you know how he loved sweets as a child.'

He drew up lists and lists of guests he would invite to meet his son – religious leaders, advisors, members of his court, prominent citizens – their numbers ran into thousands.

Mother watched all this with a wry smile. Grandma scolded her, 'Yashodhara, how can you just sit there, smiling like that? Come and help me with the preparations.'

'Silks and treasures meant little to him before, Mother Gotami. Now, he cares not whether he dines in palaces or rests in a little hut. They are all the same to him.' Tears streaked Mother's face, yet her eyes glowed with pride.

I gaped at everything that was happening around me, comprehending none of it. But my heart beat with excitement too. All I could think was – finally, at long last, I would see my father! I too would have a father to play and horse around with, like all the other lads in the city."

As I recalled the excitement of that day, Shravana shifted closer to me, as if to catch my words before anyone else. His knees drawn up and that little chin resting on his cupped hands, eyes wide with anticipation – was this not me, waiting to catch my first glimpse of Father?

"One day, Grandfather was informed that 300 saffron-clad *bhikkhus* had arrived in the capital. He rushed out and leaped into his carriage. I ran, along with the womenfolk, up to the highest terrace in the Palace to watch out for Father. We were stunned by the event that unfolded before us.

We could see monks begging silently in front of a humble dwelling. Their leader had a noble bearing, despite his shorn head and frayed robe. Grandfather stopped his carriage and began approaching him. Just then, this monk accepted a food offering from a poor woman, bowing to her in deep gratitude. As he turned to move on, he saw Grandpa approaching.

He handed his bowl to another monk and walked with slow, dignified steps towards Grandpa, who was stumbling and rushing to cover the short distance as fast as possible. As they came closer, it looked like Grandpa would hug him but he hesitated. And then I saw him join his hands and bow to the monk, as we would to a venerable one.

Mother spoke softly in my ear, 'That is your father, Rahula. Go and meet him!'

I stared at her for a bewildered moment. Then I bolted out, stopping only when I had flung myself straight into Father's arms.

That moment is so clearly imprinted in my mind. I can recall the lean firmness of Father's hands as he reached out and held me tight. He stroked my hair and the top of my head tingled for days after that.

'Mother has told me you have a special inheritance for me. What is it Father, please give it to me,' I pleaded.

He smiled with infinite compassion and patted my cheek. The picture is etched in my memory – the sight of my father, so elegant, regal and soft-spoken, yet so lean and simple. I had expected a giant of a man, in shining armour, riding in on a great horse with wings, with an entourage of angels and trumpeters leading the way. And instead, here was a quiet assembly of monks in saffron robes, heads shaven, begging bowls in hand, with my father leading them.

Grandpa immediately started to scold Father:

'Why must you beg like this? You are a Prince of the Sakya clan. You could have come straight to the Palace for your meal. Why did you not come to see your family first?'

Father explained gently that he could no longer dwell with us at the Palace.

'I am a *bhikkhu* now, Father. I belong with the Sangha, the community I travel with. Begging is part of our spiritual practice. It helps us develop humility and recognize the equality of all beings. We are as grateful for an offering from a humble home as we would be for a banquet at the Palace.'

I knew then that I wanted to be like Father. His quiet words had left Grandpa speechless and had stirred my little being. My father, prince and heir to the Sakya throne, was a *bhikkhu* now, begging quietly in front of the dwellings in his own kingdom! And yet, what radiance, what dignity shone forth from him. There was a serenity about him that I had not seen in anyone before. His voice was soft and each word was measured, creating an awed silence around him.

Mother and Grandmother broke down when they met Father. He bowed silently and thanked them for allowing him to leave in search of his quest. Mother sobbed quietly as he said that it was her special strength that gave him comfort.

'I knew you would understand when I left you and the baby,' he told her.

Grandfather invited Father and all the *bhikkhus* for a meal at the Palace. I was allowed to serve them the fragrant rice Mother had specially prepared, along with warm curry. They ate in complete silence and, awed by them, so did the other guests. I had never seen Palace officials at such a loss. They did not know which way to step and what to say. No one had ever heard of a Crown Prince who had walked away into the forest and had returned as a great spiritual teacher, eating only from his begging bowl. They were silent, afraid of even rustling their fine silken clothes! I was so amused I wanted to burst into laughter. Mother gave me a stern look and I bent my head to hide my smile.

Father then addressed the assembly. As he sat in the lotus position, his whole being was filled with light. He looked at each one of us with his immensely compassionate gaze and explained what the Way of Awakening was. All I understood was that my Father, the Buddha, knew how to make the whole world beautiful and magically alive.

Father's teachings attracted many young men to the Sangha, including my uncle, Nanda. I envied him because he could spend all his time with Father at Nigrodha Park, where Granfather had built some dwellings for the monks. So one day, when Mother permitted me to visit Father, I asked if I, too, could join the Sangha. To the utter surprise of everyone around, Father agreed.

'He is too young,' said one monk.
'Our vows are too harsh for a child his age,' said another.

'Ordain him as a novice and let him serve the senior monks,' said Father. He asked Sariputta to take charge. My hair was shaved off and Sariputta shortened one of his own robes to fit me. I was given a begging bowl and was ordained in a simple ceremony, where I chanted,

Buddham sharanam gacchami
Dhamman sharanam gacchami
Sangham sharanam gacchami

These were the three refuges; they meant:

I take refuge in the Buddha
I take refuge in the Dhamma
I take refuge in the Sangha."

And there ended the session for that day. We agreed we would continue after the next day's meal.

LESSONS FROM A FATHER

W hat has got into the monks?" I wondered, as I walked towards the meditation hall. They were behaving very strangely – some were hiding behind bushes and others were standing in peculiar positions, frozen like statues. As they saw me approach, however, they shuffled together into an embarrassed group, bowing to me in apology. A young voice piped up,

"I was teaching them the game of thieves and sentries!" Shravana explained, with a wide grin.

"We must locate his uncle," I said to a senior monk.

Shravana looked hesitant and worried. "I'll never do it again, Venerable Rahula, please don't send me away until our story is done!"

One could not but be amused by this chirruping lad! As I smiled he bowed gratefully and arranged cushions in the hall for the monks, so that we could all sit down and resume the story-telling session.

"You said you joined the Sangha and became a novice monk. Life in the forest must have been so different from Palace life," he said.

"Well, it was a new chapter that started in my life. I would wake up with the monks before dawn. As they practised meditation, I chased away the crows that disturbed the silence in the grove. I was taught how to meditate, though I did not practice as rigorously. And I was a naughty little fellow! Sometimes, I opened my eyes just a little bit and watched the squirrels instead of my breath! Luckily, I got to eat more than the monks did – they ate only once a day but thanks to my teacher, Sariputta, I was allowed two meals.

My most precious moments were when I was allowed to sit in front of Father as he addressed the monks. In the early years, I understood little of what he said. I was thrilled just to sit there. His eyes and smile reflected the immense calm and beauty of the Liberation that he had achieved. His love and compassion reached out to all beings. Many lay people came to meet him too, often with troubled minds. Just one look from his serene eyes would dissolve years of distress, conflict and turmoil. They would break down in tears of gratitude and love for the Master.

Though I was never lonely in the company of the *bhikkhus*, I often missed Mother and her soft touch. And so, at times, I would weep quietly at night, afraid of being heard or of being found out. Father treated me like any other *bhikkhu*, taking care to ensure that I was not getting special treatment just because I was his son. But I was young then and sometimes I wished dearly that I could clamber into his lap at night or that he would come with me to play in the forest.

I remember one morning, though, when he took me with him for walking meditation. We walked in silence till we reached the banks of the river. He sat down on a large boulder and motioned to me to do likewise. Dawn broke and the birds began to chirp. The river turned a deep blue. As we gazed upon this scene, some birds alighted nearby, foraging for worms and seeds. A kingfisher dived into the river, a flash of brilliant blue, flying away triumphantly with a struggling fish gripped firmly in its beak. Squirrels and rabbits emerged, their little noses twitching as they sensed our presence. Father and I stayed absolutely still, observing the little drama that Nature was unfolding before us. I watched transfixed as a row of red ants began a long, arduous journey, dragging a dead beetle to some secret location.

Then he spoke:

'Observe the interdependence of all creatures, Rahula. One cannot do without the other. The sun must rise for there to be light. Light sustains life on earth. Seeds germinate and become trees. Birds live on the trees. They must hunt to feed themselves and their young. The large creatures eat the small creatures, which, in turn, eat smaller ones. Finally though, all creatures die and return to the earth.

Observe the river, Rahula. Water flows endlessly in the river, carrying in it the minerals from high mountain peaks that we cannot even see from here. The river carries in itself the story of thousands of tiny creatures that took birth, lived and died, as it flowed from the mountaintops to the sea, miles away. On the way, it nourishes the fields and rice grows, feeding the farmer as well as the town folk. The minerals from the mountaintop are contained in the rice, even as the sunlight is contained in the leaf of the Peepal tree over there.

All beings are hewn of the same building blocks, Rahula. The most venomous snake is as afraid of being attacked as a young calf is. Sickness, old age and death affect the wealthy as well as the poorest beggar. Separation from loved ones causes the same pain. A soldier's wife prays for his life and scans the horizon for a glimpse of her husband each day, just as you long for a glimpse of your Mother and grandparents.

So recognise the equality of all beings, son. Respect all beings, for each one is deserving of it, just as your Mother is.' "

Shravana and the *bhikkhus* were moved by these words. I had been too. My little heart had expanded in ecstasy, at being part of such a great cosmos. Listening to Father, I felt a sense of belonging with the Universe – this was my home. All these creatures were just like me, I thought. They get hungry, they like to play and they hurt when the hunter's arrow pierces their body. They too go through birth, development and decay.

I paused for a while and we meditated there, under the rain tree. We went for a walk by the river and there, on the sandy, shallow beach, I continued my tale. I was enjoying it as much as the little lad was!

"I travelled with the *bhikkhus* of the Sangha and saw many new places. We went to Magadha and I saw Venuvana, the great Bamboo Forest monastery that the monks had built in the park that King Bimbisara had donated. I had not realised until then how useful the humble bamboo was. Slashed together with strong ropes, it made the walls of huts. With holes punched through a short piece, it could transform breath into heavenly music.

34

When I was still a very young novice, I returned one night to my hut after Father's Dhamma talk. I found my robe and bowl outside and my hut occupied by a senior monk. I had no option but to spend the night in the washroom. It was not so bad at first but then a huge storm whipped up and rain started lashing the structure. I stayed huddled in a corner, trying my best to sleep. Soon, I realised I had company! The burrows of all the creeping, crawling creatures had been flooded with water and a variety of little monsters were rushing in to the washroom, to shelter for the night. I could not bear it anymore – I rushed out of there crying, and, to my astonishment, I found Father outside. He called my name and I clung to him, sobbing till my fears subsided. He stroked my head and allowed me to spend that night in his hut.

But there were rough lessons to be learned, too. I got my share of reprimands throughout my boyhood!"

"Did the Buddha actually spank you?" Shravana asked, in some surprise.

"Oh no, he never so much as raised his voice. Whether a sermon or a reprimand, his compassion never waned. And I can assure you that made his scolding much, much harder to endure.

One morning, I didn't feel like doing my regular chores and when I saw Sariputta was busy, I ran away to the forest to play. I had a wonderful time. I picked some berries and climbed up into the low branches of a tree to enjoy my snack. I pelted the squirrels with the seeds when I was through and laughed aloud as they ran away, chattering angrily at me with their bristling tails held high.

This was great, I thought. A well-earned break from the daily grind of cleaning the huts, cleaning the basins, filling drinking water from the river, washing my robes – how tedious that became sometimes.

It was almost noon when I went back to where we were staying, at the Ambalatthika Park, just near the Bamboo Forest. When Sariputta asked where I had been, I made up a long-winded story. He said nothing and I drew a deep breath of relief. All through that day, however, in order to cover up for that one lie, I had to tell many more lies.

A prank that I loved to play was to send visiting monks and lay people on a wild goose chase when they came to visit Father. If they arrived when he was away practising walking meditation, I gave them complicated directions to where he was. They would wander helplessly all over the monastery and I would follow them stealthily, delighting in their confusion. Then I'd narrate these escapades to the younger *bhikkhus*, laughing till I got a bellyache.

Father was staying at the Bamboo Forest then and one day, he came to visit us. I was very excited and I ran to fetch a low stool for him to sit on. I adored him and treasured every opportunity I got to sit by him. But that day, I would have run away, had I only known what was in store!

He asked me to get some water in a basin so he could wash his feet. After he was done, he asked,

'Can anyone drink this water now, Rahula?'

'No, Father,' I replied, 'It is dirty and no one **can** drink it.'

'By speaking untruth, Rahula, your mind is as defiled as this water is,' he said.

Then, pouring the water out, he asked again, 'Can this basin now be used to fill water for drinking?'

'No Father, it cannot. It, too, has become dirty.'

'So it is with you, Rahula. You have taken the vows of a novice monk and you wear the robes of the Sangha, yet you have become as unclean as this basin.'

My heart was filled with regret but he would not stop.

'Now, if I were to break this basin, would it matter Rahula?'

'No Father, it is merely an earthen basin and it really doesn't matter to anyone if it breaks.'

'You are as worthless as this basin Rahula, when you play your pranks on visiting monks and lay people. No one will care about you, just as no one would really care if this basin is shattered right now.'

I was overcome with remorse and hot tears scalded my cheeks, but he was not done yet!

'Tell me, do you know why we use a mirror?' he asked.

'To see our reflection, Father,' I replied, my head hanging low, my voice barely audible.

'Look upon your thoughts, words and actions, just as a person would look into a mirror, Rahula.'

That was the first scolding I received from Father. I had never heard him speak a sharp word before and I sobbed in Sariputta's arms long after he was gone.

'It is not for you to feel guilty that he spoke thus,' my gentle Master told me. 'Just as a young sapling needs support and pruning for it to grow up straight and tall, so it is with young boys, Rahula!'

Once we were on our way to a village near Savatthi, to beg for our daily meal. I spotted a beautiful mountain eagle swooping down from the skies, in search of prey. The bird fascinated me and my mind strayed. We had lots of kites flying near the Palace at Kapilavatthu. Grandfather knew I was fascinated by birds and had promised I could have a falcon when I grew older.

I wondered, 'What if Father had not become the Buddha? Would I have been in the Palace still...?'

Though Father was walking up ahead of me, he turned and asked, 'Are you observing your breath, Rahula? Are you walking in mindfulness?'

I could not even reply. I merely hung my head, embarrassed and repentant.

'We observe our breath to maintain mindfulness. We practice meditation not just in the monastery but during walking, during begging as well. Observe your breath and your thoughts will not wander.'

I could not bear being corrected like that, in front of all the *bhikkhus*. I broke away from the group and sulked alone in the forest. A young monk came to join me but I shooed him away. On the way back, a couple of them shared their meal with me and when we were finished eating, Sariputta told me Father wished to see me. I was torn up inside, feeling remorse and afraid of what lay in store for me. I wished Mother were here to shield me from the ticking off that was definitely coming my way.

Luckily, Sariputta came along. I bowed to Father as I entered his hut. Tears were choking my throat and threatening to break free at the edges of my eyelids. He seemed not to notice.

'Look upon this earth, Rahula,' he said. 'Whether we place beautiful objects on it, like flowers and incense, or if we dirty it with excrement, it receives everything, without clinging or aversion. Observe the water, Rahula. We wash our dirty linen in it, we wash ourselves with it. Whether we pour milk into it or we wash our dirty feet in it, it accepts both, with neither clinging nor aversion. It remains immense and flowing, capable of nourishing and purifying.

Learn from fire too. Fire burns all things, without distinction. It does not stop to judge whether they are pure or impure, it merely exercises its power to burn, purify and transform. Dwell upon the nature of the air, too, Rahula. It bears along all fragrances, pleasant or unpleasant, again, making no distinction between them.

Just so, when pleasant or unpleasant thoughts arise in your mind, do not cling to them. Recognise them as just thoughts and allow them to pass through you. We practice meditation to awaken and liberate this mind, so that it ever observes and accepts, free from clinging as well as aversion. We live as monks, observing the rules of the Sangha, as this way of life serves to deepen our practice. And what is this way, Rahula?

We practice loving kindness, to overcome anger. Loving kindness has the capacity to rid people of unhappiness, without expecting anything in return. We practice compassion, to overcome cruelty. Compassion is the salve for the suffering of all beings and it nourishes your own heart. We practice sympathetic joy, to overcome hatred. Sympathetic joy allows us to participate in the happiness and success of others, without experiencing jealousy. We practice non-attachment, to overcome prejudice. We look upon all things with equanimity.

Do not create barriers between yourself and others, Rahula, for they are not separate.'

He then taught me to observe my breath.

'Breathing in, become aware that you are breathing in. Breathing out, become aware that you are breathing out. Focus on awareness of breath, for it helps to develop concentration and allows you to dwell in mindfulness. Mindfulness deepens understanding and with true

Understanding, you can awaken the Buddha nature that resides in all beings.'

It was one of those rare occasions when I had received instruction directly from Father. How I treasured that moment through my life.

I became a fully-ordained monk when I turned 20. Sariputta performed the ceremony and I took the more stringent vows of a *bhikkhu*. As the years passed, I saw Father less and less. Sariputta guided my practice. The depth of his understanding of the Buddha's teaching was legendary. At the evening discourse, it was as if the Buddha himself was giving the talk. After a while, he began to encourage me to give a Dhamma talk and when I was ready, I was given charge of a batch of young *bhikkhus*– I became their teacher and guided their practice. And then I too began to travel to distant lands, preaching the wisdom and compassion of the Buddha."

"Don't you miss your family, Venerable Rahula?" Shravana enquired.

"The entire human race is my family now, Shravana. No one is less or more special. My Mother Yashodhara and Grandmother Gotami reside in the hearts of all mothers and grandmothers. The Buddha lives in my heart and in the hearts of all the *bhikkhus* of the Sangha. He dwells in you too.

We tend to love only those that are 'ours'. We are moved greatly when 'our' loved ones suffer. But we tend to be indifferent, or even hostile, when suffering befalls those who we do not consider part of our family. When you walk the

Path of Dhamma, you understand that all beings yearn for loving kindness and compassion. And you discover that within each heart is a wellspring of infinite love. The more you give, the more you find you have to give."

Shravana was somewhat tearful when Kapila led him away that evening, to his uncle's home. The *bhikkhus* gathered around, comforting him.

"Don't worry, even if your uncle does not permit you now, you can join the Sangha when you become 20 year old. And till then, we will come and visit whenever we are passing this way!"

He managed to muster up a shaky smile. We watched as the lad walked through the forest, on his way home.

Book II: Triguna
The Charioteer

KING BIMBISARA

King Bimbisara ruled over the kingdom of Magadha, which lay south of the great river Ganga. It was a prosperous kingdom and the King was a just and generous ruler. In keeping with the tradition of Kings, he indulged, occasionally, in skirmishes with his neighbours, notably with the Licchavi nobles. However, a chance encounter with a monk of noble aspect made a profound impression on the King and a series of quiet events began to transform Magadha's society.

Allow me to introduce myself – I am Triguna, King Bimbisara's charioteer.

My story begins on a fine spring morning. We were returning to the capital, Rajagaha, from a routine tour of the outposts. We passed a monk begging in the streets, a picture of such grace and nobility that the King halted, just to observe him. Upon enquiry, we found he had made a dwelling on the hillside outside the capital.

The next morning King Bimbisara instructed me to take him there. Now I too was curious about this man. I secured the horses firmly and climbed up a Jambu tree for a better view. I watched the King bow and introduce himself. And then he made the monk an amazing offer:

"Your bearing is that of a nobleman, kind sire! It shines through the patches in your robe and lends grace to that begging bowl in your hands. You should be creating and enjoying wealth. Please, come with me, join my court as my special advisor. I am willing to build you a palace and share my kingdom with you."

Obviously, I had not gauged the depth of the King's interest in this monk. But I was not prepared for his reply either:

"Your offer is generous, but I cannot accept it, Your Highness. I have become a monk to seek a way out of the suffering of old age, sickness and death. And I have left behind the lavish comforts of a Palace because they obstruct one's pursuit of the spiritual path. Your Majesty, I am Siddhartha, son of King Shuddhodana, of the Sakya kingdom."

"I am intrigued that a son of such an illustrious warrior family has become a monk," King Bimbisara remarked. "And in the prime of youth too! Only when confronted by sickness, and imminent death, do men turn to a life of spirituality. Why must you pursue spiritual life now, Venerable Sire?"

The monk explained,

"I do not wish to waste my youth leading the comfortable life of a Prince. As we grow old, senility and sickness are certain. Death hovers around us constantly, striking at will, without warning. I want to find the Way before that. And so I have left behind my parents, my wife and a young son, to become a monk and find the path that leads to Liberation."

I listened intently to the silence, as the King mulled over the young monk's words.

"When you find the Way, please come back to our kingdom and instruct us, O noble monk," said the King finally, as he bowed and took his leave. I scrabbled down from my perch and darted back to the carriage.

It was a very pensive King I took back to the Palace. I was deeply moved too – I could not speak that day.

You see, I am not a learned man; I was born to be a charioteer. And I had been a good charioteer, I believed. I loved my horses and I took good care of them. I kept the carriage polished, the wheels oiled and ready to roll, be it noon or night. Two little children and my wife, Nandini, comprised my family. They filled my life with joy, though my wife did complain about the equine odour embedded in my pores. All in all, the good Lord had bestowed his generosity on me and I had no reason to complain.

Surely life must have been even more pleasant for Prince Siddhartha. It was every man's dream to be born a Prince and yet, here was one who had actually abandoned it all, to spend his time contemplating under trees and begging for his food. He said he had a wife and child and he left them behind, to look for a way out of human suffering – but was there really such a way? Where would he find it?

His quiet presence haunted me for a few days. Then the seasons changed and he faded from memory.

47

It was many monsoons later that a large community of monks appeared in Rajagaha. In orange robes and shorn heads, they begged quietly for their morning meal, at the doors of the rich and poor alike. We were mystified by their calm countenances and while making our offering, we asked about their order.

"We are members of the Sangha founded by the Buddha, the Enlightened One. He has found the way out of human suffering and preaches the Four Noble Truths and the Noble Eightfold Path," one of them replied.

A thrill of anticipation ran through my body as I heard this.

"Was this Buddha the Sakya Prince, Siddhartha Gautama, before he became a monk?" I asked.

"That is so," replied the monk.

I rushed to the Palace and asked to be taken to the King at once. "Your Majesty, Prince Siddhartha has found the Great Way of Liberation! He is now called the Buddha, the Enlightened One! He has arrived on the outskirts of the capital with at least a thousand disciples," I announced, as the ministers stared in surprise.

The King's face lit up in excitement. He told me to get the chariot ready and asked Queen Videhi to accompany him, along with their son, Prince Ajatasattu. He ordered all the Brahmins and intellectuals of his court to accompany him and a vast entourage soon arrived at the Palm Forest, where the monks were camping. Many officials were sceptical, however, for Enlightenment was a tall claim and this monk seemed rather young. "Another hoax," they murmured amongst themselves, but they had to humour the King.

The Buddha greeted the King warmly. The monks bowed and graciously offered folded robes as seats and cushions to the guests. The King requested him to address the assembly. I had, as before, decided to be included in the audience. As I looked for a suitable tree to climb, a young monk offered me his cushion to sit on. I gulped and sat down, misty-eyed at the honour.

The Buddha sat serene in the lotus position, his hands in gentle repose in his lap. Although I had had only a glimpse of the monk Siddhartha, this man who addressed the assembly was not he. The monk had truly undergone a transformation. He seemed radiant, just suffused with light.

He gazed at us in silence, the stillness of his being reaching out to us too. I felt my senses becoming keener. Each lilting note of the bulbul's song rang in my heart with intense clarity. Each leaf, each fluff of a floating feather was etched in sharp focus. But when he began to speak, a clear, sweet voice was all I heard.

"Human suffering results from wrong beliefs and incorrect understanding of the nature of existence. When we practice meditation to calm our minds, we are able to look deeply into the nature of all phenomena. We gain Understanding, which helps us overcome the ignorance that leads to sorrow, anxiety, fear and jealousy. In their place, we find love and compassion for all beings.

Only when we have cleansed ourselves of these defilements and freed ourselves from the shackles of ignorance can we truly experience the many splendours this universe has to offer us. And offer us it does, in abundance. Observe how the sun rises in the eastern sky, day after day, after yet another day. Sit by a stream and listen how delightfully it chortles past obstacles, ever onwards on its way to the sea. Each day, new life springs forth from this earth. And who are we, in truth, but an expression of this springing forth?

To gain true Understanding, we lead the simple, wholesome lives of monks. But it may not be possible for all to adopt monastic life. There are precepts and practices you can observe that would enable you to lead peaceful lives, while yet conducting the activities of householders, businessmen, palace nobles and traders.

There are five precepts lay disciples should observe.

The first precept is, do not kill. All beings fear death. No matter how repulsive the insect or how poisonous the snake, it deserves to live, to go its own way. Nurture this compassion in your hearts, let it form the basis of all your relationships and you will become a source of great comfort to everyone around you.

The second precept is, do not steal. We must respect the right of a person to enjoy the fruits of his own labour. They should not be stolen from him, nor should he be cheated out of them, by connivance and treachery. Ensure the labourer has been rewarded justly for his work. Do not amass a fortune yourself, while still keeping him in penury.

The third precept, is do not engage in sexual misconduct. Mutual faith and trust are essential for peaceful environs in which to raise your children. A happy family builds prosperous nations. Nourish this virtue amongst men and refrain from indulging in the company of courtesans and concubines, for it violates this precept.

The fourth precept is, do not speak untruths. Words have the power to create great unhappiness, so be careful when you speak and ensure that you have created correct understanding. We cause great harm to others when we deliberately use words to generate confusion and ambiguity. We know well how words have led to wars and killings. Let us, instead, use the power of speech to create harmony and understanding among all beings.

The fifth precept is, do not indulge in alcohol and other intoxicants. They cloud your senses and warp your mind. They hamper the practice of meditation and prevent you from observing phenomena with clarity. Therefore, abstain from intoxicants at all times.

Entire lifetimes can be spent chasing the pleasures the senses afford. Edifices are built around those who acquire wealth and power. Yet, the truly wealthy one is he who is free of desire, who has awakened to reality and who knows the secret of deathless existence."

As I heard the Buddha speak, I thought that this Path must be for others, for the learned ones, to follow. How could a charioteer aspire to attain this Awakening? As though to answer me, he continued,

"All beings carry the seeds of Enlightenment within. What is required is diligent effort. Men are not differentiated by birth, caste or occupation. Men are differentiated by their actions, by their understanding of the Truth, by their commitment to the Dhamma.

Prayer and rituals can offer but respite. To be truly Liberated, one has to make strenuous efforts to confront reality. That is only possible when you observe the precepts and calm the mind with meditation. As the agitated, random wandering of the mind ceases, you awaken to the true nature of your existence and you are Liberated from suffering!

This Path is not for the lazy and the merely curious. Nor is it an easy discipline to follow. That is why the monks live and practice in a community – the Sangha. *Bhikkhus* need the encouragement and support of fellow travellers on this Way."

Many in the assembly had questions to ask of him. I realised I was in the presence of the Prince among sages, the most noble among men. He had said we could all aspire to his Awakening – I felt humble and unworthy. Yet I knew I was going to walk his Path as best I could. For all I wanted now was to serve this Teacher.

WHAT IS ENLIGHTENMENT

The Buddha stayed in the Palm Forest for many weeks and his sermons attracted lay people as well as intellectuals. The King himself asked to be accepted as a lay disciple. He donated the Bamboo Forest, Venuvana, for the establishment of a monastery. This was the first time that the Sangha had received such a donation. The Buddha accepted graciously and started the practice of the monsoon retreat.

"From now on, we will not travel during the monsoon. Many creatures come out as their homes get flooded and we end up killing them underfoot as we travel. *Bhikkhus* also find it hard to stay dry in the forests and fall sick often. We will use this season to congregate in Venuvana – it can be a period for rigorous practice and *bhikkhus* can use the time for more intensive guidance from their masters," he declared.

I, too, asked to be ordained as a lay disciple. My free moments were spent in helping the *bhikkhus* build simple dwellings in the monastery. We cleared pathways, dug wells and built washrooms. The Master's hut was like all others, with bare walls and a thatched roof. Perhaps we could place a bed there, I suggested. No, said the *bhikkhus*, we do not sleep on high, comfortable beds. At least some cushions against the bare walls, I pleaded. Yet they shook their heads. If I had had my own way, I would have placed oil lamps on the path leading to his door and made his hut fragrant with incense sticks and flowers.

"But it *is* a Fragrant Chamber, do you not see that Triguna?" they said. As I walked home a gentle shower sprayed the earth. Turning my face upwards, I let the rain wash the warm moistness from my eyes.

In the years that followed, the Buddha would often visit the monastery at the Bamboo Forest and stay through the monsoon retreat. He was also fond of visiting the Gijjhakuta Mountain, which was also known as Vulture Peak. The King had a hut built there for the Buddha and for some of his senior disciples, like Sariputta and Moggallana.

The Sangha attracted disciples from all walks of life. Orange clad *bhikkhus* were now a familiar sight in the streets of Rajagaha. Many lay disciples donated robes and medicines to the Sangha. Along with other lay disciples, I too made meal offerings to the *bhikkhus*. I felt honoured to be able to serve these quiet, gracious men.

The King was a frequent visitor to Vulture Peak, consulting the Buddha on matters of state and family. He wanted to rule his people in the spirit of Dhamma, he said. Sometimes, he would go even if the Buddha was not staying there. He said he experienced calm and quietude on Vulture Peak.

The King was sitting outside the Buddha's hut on one such visit. I stood by a rock, etching patterns on it with a rusty nail. We watched the sun make its glorious exit behind the hills. Birds squabbled shrilly over choice perches for the night. A solitary egret flew past, calling anxiously to its mate. Wispy tendrils of wood smoke began escaping from thatched roofs in the valley below. Bells tinkled and cattle lowed, as cowherds coaxed the laggards on. Amidst the sounds of homecoming, I had a fleeting glimpse of timelessness.

"Where did the Buddha acquire such priceless wisdom, Your Majesty?" I asked of the King. "Is this what is written in the ancient texts?"

"The Buddha recites a poetry all his own, Triguna!" the King replied. "He did go to two great Masters after leaving home. They taught him how to attain high levels of concentration in meditation practice, but he still had not found a way out of human suffering. So he set off on his own and practised severe asceticism, along with five companions. But then he embarked on such extreme austerities that his companions could not keep up with him. He would eat just one grain of rice a day. He would meditate long nights in fearsome forests, not moving even when hungry beasts howled nearby. His body had become gaunt and wasted, his hair came off in tufts and he was wracked with pain, yet he persevered."

"I cannot even think on an empty stomach, Your Majesty! Is the great Truth realised only by starving oneself so?" I asked, in horrified awe.

King Bimbisara stared for a moment and then burst out laughing. "Triguna, monks practice asceticism to quell desire, which is rooted in the body. But the monk Siddhartha realised that just as wealth and opulence hampered spiritual pursuit, extreme asceticism did not guarantee the dawn of wisdom either. By then, though, it was almost too late. One day, he collapsed in exhaustion as he emerged from his bath in the river Neranjara. A young girl, Sujata, revived him by feeding him rice-milk. That day he gave up the extreme austerities and decided to focus on meditation again.

His companions went away in disgust, when they saw him going to the village to seek alms. And the monk Siddhartha practised alone. After seven weeks of intense meditation under the Peepal tree, on the full moon night of *Vesakha*, he attained Enlightenment."

"What *is* Enlightenment, Your Majesty?"

"I don't know, Triguna," the King sighed. "I have wondered too. I suspect it is something words cannot capture and contain. You can see he is a lamp unto himself. He seems to dwell on another plane, like a god. Yet he insists he is only what all men can also strive to become! He seems aloof, yet he can see right through into your innermost reality. He moves in this world untouched by sorrow, anger or doubt, yet none is denied his immense compassion. He has travelled beyond time, but he is completely immersed in each moment.

When he says we are like waves on an ocean, now arising, now falling – my heart thrills at the poetry, Triguna. But in him, the teaching is alive. It breathes and resonates in each particle of his being. In him, the Dhamma is unfolded and preserved with exquisite grace and purity. Such is Enlightenment, perhaps."

TURNING THE WHEEL OF DHAMMA

Venerable Sariputta gazed at the assembly of monks and lay disciples and asked, "What shall we discuss this evening?"

It was the weekly Dhamma talk at Venuvana and King Bimbisara was in attendance. So was I. We looked forward to listening to the Venerable Sariputta elaborate on the Master's teachings. They said that his understanding of the Dhamma was as deep and true as the Master's.

"Venerable Sariputta, please elaborate on the first sermon of the Master after his Enlightenment," the King requested.

Venerable Sariputta nodded in agreement and spoke:

"After Enlightenment, the Master was actually not inclined to speak at all. He was worried that no one would be able to comprehend his teaching, so subtle and beyond reason was his Awakening. For a week he meditated quietly thus, in the forest near Uruvela. Then he thought his teachers, Master Alara Kalama and Master Uddaka Ramaputta, would be able to grasp his message, for they were ready. But alas, both were no more. That is when he sought out his former companions, the five ascetics. They received the Master's first sermon, which he called 'Setting in Motion the Wheel of Dhamma.'

It contains the Four Noble Truths he had realised on the night of his Enlightenment.

Bhikkhus, all of us learn the Four Noble Truths when we are ordained. Yet, many of us treat the first sermon as something only the novice monks should dwell on, seeking, instead, to engage our minds in metaphysical debates about the nature of this universe. You should know, *bhikkhus*, that the depth of wisdom contained in the first sermon is enough to guide us to Liberation. Let us dwell on this wisdom today.

The first Noble Truth, the Buddha said, is the existence of suffering. And truly, reflect on this life, *bhikkhus*. Is there any respite from suffering? We step into this world crying, for no child wants to emerge from the warm comfort of its mother's womb into the harsh and cold world outside. Death, too, is heralded by pain and suffering. Between these two events is a string of moments we call life. And life is a constant struggle to be happy. We have all experienced the pain of separation from our loved ones. Which one of us has been spared the pain of not having what we desire and having what we despise? King, noble, trader or beggar you may be, yet each one experiences suffering.

Dwell again on what the Master has said. The Buddha said, '*There is suffering.*' Reflect deeply upon this, *bhikkhus* and you will realise that suffering is a state that arises from ignorance and incomplete understanding. It arises when we look upon phenomena with this grasping, clinging mind that is trapped in the notion of the Self. 'Oh, how I suffer so!' is our constant refrain. But when we dwell upon the Master's teaching we realise that phenomena, by themselves, are colourless. Like water. They just exist. They do not contain the ability to create either happiness or suffering."

"Venerable Sariputta, can you explain that a little more?" King Bimbisara requested.

"I will elaborate. Take the example of the *bhikkhus* who came from wealthy homes. They faced difficulty in living with just one meal a day and owning only three robes, as is the practice of the Sangha. There was suffering in making the change. But understand this, *bhikkhus* – having just three robes did not create the suffering. It is your own mind that compares and feels the lack from what was before – then you suffer. Having three robes is just that – having three robes. Having to clean your hut is also just that – a task to be performed. Suffering is created by the mind, when it looks upon something as favourable or unfavourable. Awaken to this reality, *bhikkhus*.

The second Noble Truth is that suffering arises from a cause. And what are the causes of suffering, *bhikkhus?* Desire and attachment, the Master said. We have all experienced desire – the desire for the pleasures afforded by fulfilment of the senses, the constant desire to either become something or to *not* become something. Reflect on desire, *bhikkhus*, for it is a force that drives us ever onward on a path that *it* charts out for us. And we rush headlong, buffeted by the accompanying achievements and miseries, always seeking more, never able to break free.

Reflecting on this desire will enable you to realise the third Noble Truth – the cessation of suffering. When the Buddha spoke at the Deer Park, only one of his former companions, Kondanna, grasped the true essence of the sermon – 'that which arises is also subject to ceasing.' That is the truth about the impermanence of all phenomena. Understanding the nature of suffering and its causes permits you to break free from ignorance into liberating knowledge. Depth of understanding brings forth the wholesome states of loving kindness and compassion towards all beings. Strive to awaken to this Understanding, *bhikkhus*.

The fourth Noble Truth points to the way, the practice, which leads to the end of suffering. The Buddha called it the Noble Eightfold Path. We walk the Noble Eightfold Path when we practice right speech, right action, right livelihood, right effort, right awareness, right concentration, right thought and right understanding.

Practising the Way is to be aware of our speech and actions, so that they ever create harmony, never causing distress or injury to another being. Along with right speech and right action, we practice right livelihood too. *Bhikkhus*, you endeavour to purify your selves for the benefit of all beings and, in return, you receive alms. Lay disciples must choose those means of serving their fellowmen that do not involve killing other beings, nor dealing in arms or intoxicants. Observing this practice fills our mind with calm and compassion and we can enter into deep states of meditation.

The Eightfold Path also involves training the mind to prevent unwholesome states from arising at all. We cannot merely be vigilant of our actions and yet allow strife and discord to rage unchecked in our minds. Truly wholesome actions emerge from a mind that is crystal clear, like a lake at dawn. For that, we practice with right effort, right awareness and right concentration.

We use our breath as a tool, to focus and concentrate our mind. As we dwell in awareness and concentration improves, thoughts do not stray from the Dhamma. With practice, we are able to prevent unwholesome thoughts from arising and should they still arise, they do not take root, they cannot build a home in our minds. They pass through and disappear.

Right understanding is crucial to attaining wisdom. It means neither clinging to narrow views about the Dhamma nor being swayed by the arguments of those who oppose the teachings of the Master. The Master has said himself – the Teaching is like the finger pointing to the moon. Do not mistake the finger for the moon, *bhikkhus!*

Practice the Noble Eightfold Path, and you will be able to awaken the Buddha nature that resides within you!"

I felt as though I had been entrusted with a rare and precious treasure. I wrapped it in silken folds of silence.

AMBAPALI

One day the King summoned me to his private chamber. He said Ambapali wished to meet the Teacher everyone was talking about. He had sought the Buddha's permission and he had agreed to meet her that afternoon. And I was assigned the task of escorting her to Venuvana.

Ambapali was the most exquisite expression of the female form. Statuesque and extremely intelligent, she could hold her own in any debate, even with men. Trained in dance and music, she had the ability to make the mere act of turning her head into a momentous event. She guarded her favours jealously, though, and it was only the most swashbuckling of nobles who dared to seek her company.

The King had long been enamoured of her. She had borne him a son, Jivaka, who was now training to be a physician. The King made generous provisions for both of them. She owned a beautiful mango grove, outside the city of Vesali.

My knees usually buckled in Ambapali's presence. I did not relish the task of taking her anywhere, for I would have to face ribald remarks from my friends. My wife would be driven to distraction at the mere mention of Ambapali's name. She would insist on checking my clothes for tell-tale strands of long hair, despite my pleas of innocence.

But I could not refuse the King and I took Ambapali to Venuvana. Her appearance caused a stir. Young *bhikkhus* lowered their eyes, unable to withstand her beauty. The Buddha was out walking and she waited gracefully on the seat that she was offered. I could not take my eyes off the delicate curve of her ankles, strung with threads of silver with tiny bells that tinkled as she moved.

The Buddha arrived and greeted her warmly. For the first time, there was not a shred of embarrassment nor lust in the eyes that gazed straight into hers. So radiant was his purity, so unsullied his compassion, that warm tears coursed down Ambapali's cheeks.

The Buddha spoke to her in his gentle voice, "Just as a flower blooms for but an instant, beauty adds lustre to your personality for a brief span of time. It fades away as you grow older. Life itself ebbs away every moment. Do not waste it in idle amusement. The fruits of meditation bring true happiness. Then you will glow with an inner beauty that will only increase as you practice deeply.

When you cast a pebble in a pond, the ripples reach far across, even to its shores. When a person starts walking this path, the benefits are experienced by the entire community around him. Practice the Way and uncover the core of bliss that lies buried within you. Let it shine forth in all your actions."

When I reached home that evening, my irate wife was discussing Ambapali with the neighbour, Lakkha, and his wife, Bala. The whole town was abuzz with the news that the Buddha had granted an audience to a courtesan. Lakkha had known me from childhood and did not bother mincing his words.

"Triguna, how can a courtesan be allowed to enter a monastery? And we hear the Buddha has even accepted an invitation to a meal offering from her! Surely even you are aware, my old friend, that monks do not walk down the path that leads to a courtesan's door?"

I spoke in icy anger:

"Rise above that narrow, chattering mind now, Lakkha. Why should any one be denied access to a monastery? It is a refuge for all beings, no matter what they do in the world outside. And the Master makes no distinction among people. All are deserving of his knowledge and compassion, for he is free from defilement. In each one, he sees only the potential of his own Awakening. He offers his knowledge without restraint, seeking only to guide all beings to Liberation. Such a one as he cares not whether he is in the company of courtesans or thieves."

And I stormed off indoors. For once, Nandini did not complain about the smell of horses that was my halo.

SUDATTA

King Pasenadi ruled over the mighty kingdom of Kosala and had family ties with the Magadhan royalty – Queen Videhi was his sister. He had been a reluctant entrant into the fold of the Buddha, but once he bowed his head, he was as loyal and steadfast in his support to the Sangha as my own King Bimbisara. It was the trader Sudatta whose efforts brought the Master to Savatthi, the capital of Kosala.

Sudatta often travelled between Savatthi and Rajagaha. He was famous for his generosity and spent large sums every year on the care of the needy. So freely did he distribute his wealth that he was better known as Anathapindika, 'the refuge of orphans.' My young nephew, Benuwa, helped him with his business in Rajagaha. It is from him that I heard this story.

It was the Buddha's second monsoon retreat in Venuvana. Sudatta was visiting Rajagaha on business and he found the entire city discussing the Buddha and his teachings. He was curious and, early one morning, he made his way to Venuvana to meet the Buddha. Sudatta begged him to explain some of his teachings. That encounter led to his becoming one of the most devoted lay disciples of the Master.

He invited the Buddha and the *bhikkhus* to Savatthi, and made haste to return and prepare a suitable dwelling place for the Sangha. Venerable Sariputta accompanied him, to help him with the planning and building of a monastery. One park seemed ideal but it belonged to Prince Jeta, who would not part with it easily.

"It is a gift from my father, I cherish it!" he said. And then added, half in jest, "You may have it if you can cover it in gold, though!"

But Sudatta was not jesting. From the next day, he began to send cartloads of gold coins to the park, his men laying them on the loamy soil. The Prince was shocked when he heard about this and rushed to meet him. He found that two-thirds of the floor had already been covered with coins. He stopped the next cartload from being spread, and said to Sudatta,

"My friend, I am indeed amazed at your sincerity. I must meet the man who inspires such devotion in you. Allow me to present the rest of the grove to you, please!"

Sudatta named the park Jetavana, after the Prince. Venerable Sariputta helped him plan simple dwellings for the *bhikkhus* and a Dhamma Hall, in which they could listen to the Buddha's sermons.

As the Buddha commenced his journey to Savatthi, Ambapali met him and invited him for a meal at her mango grove. On her way back, however, she was waylaid by the nobles of the Licchavi clan. They had heard of her meeting with the Buddha and they mocked her, saying:

"Don't waste your youth and beauty serving that monk. You were made for pleasure – come with us, we can provide the wealth and happiness of your dreams!"

But Ambapali lashed out with her biting wit, "It does not behove nobility to make such a display of ignorance. Do you really believe your bits of gold can build the pathway to heaven? Dusty may be the Path of the Buddha, but truly wealthy are those who tread softly behind him. I will not go with you, even if you pave the way to my house with gold!"

The nobles were taken aback and curious, now, about this monk. They went to the forest where the *bhikkhus* were camping and asked to meet the Buddha. He spoke to them about the Four Noble Truths and the Noble Eightfold Path. He spoke of wisdom and compassion and the seeds of Liberation that all beings carried within them. He explained how incorrect understanding caused untold suffering and that eliminating ignorance allowed one to lead a life filled with peace and equanimity.

The nobles experienced an unfolding in their hearts as they listened to the Exalted One. They invited him for a meal offering too and asked to be accepted as lay disciples. They promised to build a *vihara* for the *bhikkhus* in Vesali, which could serve as a place for dwelling and practising the Way.

The Buddha reached Savatthi to a warm welcome from Prince Jeta and Sudatta. He praised the efforts of Sudatta and the humble trader glowed with gratitude. Many people came to hear the Buddha speak that evening. Queen Mallika, who had heard so much about the Buddha from her son,

67

also came with her daughter, Princess Vajiri. King Pasenadi, however, refused to be drawn in.

"How can one so young be Enlightened?" he asked. But as the days went by, the Buddha's discourses at Jetavana became the topic of discussion among his ministers as well. Despite his scepticism, then, the King found himself going to Jetavana to meet the Buddha.

"There are many teachers who are older than you. They have a large number of disciples and are well respected by all. Yet they do not claim to have attained Enlightenment. How are you able to do so?" he asked.

"But you must realise, your Majesty, that Enlightenment does not depend on age," replied the Buddha. "There are four things that should be respected, regardless of how small or young they are – a prince or warrior of noble birth, a snake, a spark and a monk. A young prince is destined to rule one day and should you treat him with disdain, he will come down on you with his royal might. A spark lives for a brief moment, but it has the ability to burn down entire forests, leaving a blackened trail where mighty trees once soared to the sky. Similarly, a snake may look very small, but you are aware its venom can kill a grown man. Just so, your Majesty, a monk may look young but it is possible for him to have attained Enlightenment."

The King was delighted with the Buddha's response. The Buddha then explained to him how it was possible for nations to be ruled without violence and persecution. It required great conviction and persistence on the part of the ruler, he said, but such effort would benefit all citizens. He had discussed this even with his own father, King Shuddhodana, he said.

"People will devote their time to doing what they are supposed to do, what they should do, when they are in a peaceful atmosphere. A nation prospers when a farmer focuses on being a good farmer and a merchant is alert and strikes good bargains. Encourage the citizens to participate in each other's lives, without distinction of caste or occupation. Share knowledge freely. Set aside a portion of wealth to improve the lot of the less fortunate. Lead by example, Your Highness and your people will follow you. Shifty, manipulative behaviour draws forth anger, fear and hatred in its wake. But with loving kindness, one is able to reach out to the most hardened criminal."

They spoke for a long time, in great detail. When it was time to leave, King Pasenadi was effusive in his praise, "How simply marvelous, how inspiring is your wisdom, Master! You explain with such ease, as if only turning upright that which was overturned."

Sudatta's efforts bore fruit. The Sangha blossomed in Kosala. Jetavana became the monastery where the Buddha spent the annual monsoon retreat. This permitted *bhikkhus* from distant places to plan and travel to Savatthi and benefit from the Buddha's personal guidance.

PRINCE AJATASATTU

The years passed, as they do, in just moments. It was getting harder to climb the steps to Vulture Peak now. The Sangha had expanded and great centres of learning had also been established in neighbouring kingdoms. After a gap of many months, the Buddha was visiting Rajagaha. I should have been celebrating his presence, but instead, I was plagued by strange fears.

My training as a charioteer had taught me to pay heed to little sounds and small dissonances. For ignoring them could mean losing a wheel or, worse still, a lame horse. And I could sense dark clouds gathering over Magadha. A harsh wind whistled through the streets, whipping up a red dust that stung our eyes and made us ill. The horses stamped fretfully in their stalls and the atmosphere seemed laden with dark, shadowy presences.

There was the monk Devadatta again, emerging from the gates leading to Prince Ajatasattu's chambers. Those two really get on famously, I thought. But was it just my imagination, or did he really have a surreptitious air about him? A cousin of the Buddha and a monk besides – why did he need to skulk around the Palace?

It's that ill wind again, I told myself, trying to shake the uneasy feeling off. Huddling in my cloak, I hurried homewards. As

I walked through the Market Street, a voice called out, "Over here, Triguna! Come, try some of these fresh rice cakes!"

It was my old friend Shriranga, the sweet-meat seller. He tended to consume a large quantity of his own wares and was a genial fellow, with a belly full of laughter.

"What is this I hear about the Sangha?" he asked, as I settled on his bench. "It seems the monk Devadatta asked the Buddha to hand over the leadership of the Sangha, saying he was now too old and feeble to lead it. How on earth did he have the nerve?"

I forgot the cakes and hurried to Venuvana, where the *bhikkhus* confirmed the story. They said Venerable Devadatta was getting increasingly upset by the respect accorded to the two gems of the Sangha, Venerables Sariputta and Moggallana. As a cousin of the Master and a senior monk, he felt he deserved to be the right hand of the Buddha. But the Buddha had snubbed him. He had told him there were many monks senior to him whom he would consider first, should he ever decide to hand over leadership of the Sangha. The *bhikkhus* were saddened by Venerable Devadatta's behaviour. He was respected within the Sangha. The revelation that he could fall prey to jealousy, after so many years with the Master, alarmed many of the young *bhikkhus*.

I had my own worries. Venerable Devadatta was fomenting trouble in the Sangha alright but what was he doing spending so much time with young Prince Ajatasattu? Their growing friendship worried me, and I decided to find out what was going on. The next time Venerable Devadatta visited the

71

Palace, I sneaked into an antechamber to the Prince's suite. What I heard made me shake with fury.

"How long will you wait to become King?" the conniving rascal asked the foolish Prince. "Of what use will it be if you ascend to the throne with bony, aching knees? The time to enjoy power and wealth is now, Your Majesty. Let us do something about the old King and ensure that you take his place before you grow older."

I saw the evil game in its entirety now! With the old King done away with and Prince Ajatasattu installed on the throne of Magadha, Venerable Devadatta could ensure that the royal patronage enjoyed by the Sangha was withdrawn, unless he was made its leader.

I walked home filled with helpless rage. Dare I reveal to the King what I had just heard? The King was devoted to his son and would never believe me. He might, in fact, send me to the gallows for making such allegations. Oh, what a wretched, powerless charioteer I was. I stumbled in my misery and narrowly missed getting knocked down by a horse-rider.

"Hey Triguna! Watch where you are going, my friend!" It was Jivaka, the physician. Here was the man I needed, he would listen to me. Disregarding his concern for my grazed shin and rapidly swelling ankle, I told him what I had learned.

Jivaka agreed that the King was blinded by his love for his son and would not listen to us. However, he rode off to Vulture Peak to inform the Buddha about the plot. Over the next few days, I waited for signs of change, but life carried on in Venuvana as before. There was nothing in the Buddha's words or actions to suggest he was aware of the treacherous intentions of his own cousin. Sick with worry, I began to leap at shadows and cry out in my sleep. Nandini made me drink vile brews recommended by the neighbour's wife but the demon that needed exorcising was walking undetected in Venuvana.

One evening, after the Dhamma talk at Venuvana, Venerable Devadatta stood up and spoke:

"Master, the *bhikkhus* of the Sangha lead very comfortable lives. We compare unfavourably with the followers of other Masters. We must introduce stricter rules in the Sangha , to truly lead a simple life. I suggest that from now on, *bhikkhus* should stay only in forests and not sleep in any roofed dwelling. They must eat only vegetarian food. They should not accept robes offered by lay disciples but, instead, wear robes sewn from discarded rags and cloth picked up from tombs and burial places. And they should never accept a meal offering at the homes of lay people."

But the Buddha did not agree.

"Devadatta, I have explained to you before – in the Sangha, we practise the Middle Path. Just as we shun a life of luxury, we do not resort to extreme measures of austerity either. This body needs to be cared for, for without it we have no receptacle for the fruits of our practice.

Bhikkhus may observe the precepts you recommend, if they so wish. But no one need be forced to observe them. The

73

bhikkhus may stay in the forest if they wish. However, they may also stay in the monastery if they wish to. They should, preferably, eat vegetarian food. However, they may consume food with meat if they are sure the animal was not killed specifically for their consumption. Over time, as people realise that *bhikkhus* prefer vegetarian food, they themselves will stop making offerings with meat. *Bhikkhus* may wear robes sewn from rags but it does not matter if they wear robes donated by lay disciples. As for accepting invitations from lay people for meals at their homes – why, that offers a means of contact and an opportunity to spread the message of the Dhamma. There is no need to stop such a practice."

Venerable Devadatta was offended. He formed a breakaway group in the Sangha, managing to gather almost 500 *bhikkhus* around him. He announced to them that though the Buddha prescribed simple living, his Sangha did not truly live by it. Finally, the Buddha announced the expulsion of Venerable Devadatta from the Sangha. But Prince Ajatasattu built new headquarters at Gayasisa for the breakaway group and extended his support to it.

This was only the first move of a treacherous plot, hatched in the dark of night. My concern for the King's safety would not let me rest. One night, I wrapped a cloak around myself and made my way to the Palace. I decided I would walk around the Palace, checking for strange movements. I could not kill, for I had to observe my precepts, but I could at least shield the King with my own body.

As I neared the Palace, two guards thundered past me on horseback, forcing me against the wall. Their urgency alarmed me and I ran towards the gates. Cloaked figures with torches were milling around, in an ominous, shadowy dance.

"Halt!" cried the guards. "What brings you here at this time of night?"
"I wish to see the King on a matter of great import. Let me in," I said.
"We have orders not to let anyone enter or leave the Palace tonight."
"Why? What has happened?" I cried anxiously.

But they would not speak, the fools! Two of the King's advisors arrived, in a cloud of dust churned up by urgent, rumbling carriage wheels. Amid the excitement and confusion, I slipped into the Palace.

I was now quite familiar with the art of eavesdropping. This time, I hid close to the King's chamber, in case he was in danger. I could see a defiant Prince Ajatasattu, held firm by the King's personal guards. The King summoned his advisors and informed them that the Prince had been caught trying to enter his bedchamber with a sword. He had confessed that he wanted to assassinate his father in order to inherit the kingdom. The King could not believe that his son harboured such murderous intentions.

"You are incapable of such convoluted thinking, Ajatasattu! Who put such evils designs into your head?"

After much coaxing, the Prince revealed that this was Devadatta's plan. The advisors were strong in their condemnation of both, the Prince and the monk:

75

"An attempt on the King's life is a serious offence, Your Majesty, deserving the harshest punishment. The Prince and the monk should pay with their lives. It is outrageous that the Sangha, of which you have been so supportive, encourages hatred and discord among members of the royal family. We should behead the entire lot of *bhikkhus!* There is no telling what further evil is being planned for the kingdom of Magadha."

The King sat quietly, observing his breath, as the Buddha had taught him. Finally, he said, "I cannot behead my own son. He has been led astray by wrong advice. As for Venerable Devadatta, he has not imbibed the Teachings and his mind is still trapped in ignorance. That is why the Buddha has expelled him from the Sangha. But weakness does not call for a sentence of such finality. Forgiveness and good counsel will guide them both back to the Path."

The next morning King Bimbisara announced that he was stepping down in favour of his son. The Palace was plunged into gloom. Ministers met in huddled groups trying to find their place in this strange political climate. King Bimbisara had reigned now for almost 52 years, having ascended to the throne when he was just 15 years old. He had earned the loyalty and admiration of his men for he was a fair and just man. His devotion to the Dhamma had further endeared him to the citizens. "Our King leads by example," they said.

No one knew what to expect from the young Prince. It was rumoured that he intended to behead anyone suspected of opposing his reign. I had visions of hanging from a noose myself, for my loyalty to the old King was well known.

King Bimbisara summoned me to his chamber that evening and asked me to convey a message to the Buddha,

"Tell him I have abdicated in favour of my son, Prince Ajatasattu. I cannot offer more detail at the moment, Triguna. But I am sure he will understand."

"I cannot leave you just now, Your Majesty. Please let me stay by your side," I begged him.

"Go!" he thundered. And I left.

The Buddha was surprised at the news. The King had always consulted him on Palace matters, before taking any action, and this was indeed a major step. The Buddha asked if anything was amiss, but I could not reveal what I knew. I was afraid to speak and in deep distress. The Buddha seemed to understand. He patted my head as I bowed before him and asked me to go back to the Palace.

Not content with the abdication, Prince Ajatasattu imprisoned his father and crowned himself King. Only Queen Videhi was allowed to meet her husband. She would carry food for her husband when she visited. In an act of pure wickedness, Ajatasattu stopped all food from being carried into the prison cell.

The citizens of Magadha watched these developments with dismay and fear.

ATTEMPTS TO KILL THE BUDDHA

Armed visitors

King Bimbisara's condition worsened by the day. Guards discovered that Queen Videhi had been smuggling food to her husband, despite her son's instructions. The crazed Ajatasattu stopped her visits altogether. I could not bear his cruelty and found it hard to swallow my own dinner. Wrapping some rice cakes in a small bundle of cloth, I set off for the prison. Its walls were tall and imposing and I stared wretchedly at the window of the King's cell. If only I could find a way of slinging the bundle in.

I did not hear the guards approaching. They had me bound in chains and hauled into the new King's chamber before I could cry for help. I pleaded with King Ajatasattu to allow the old King some food, at least once a day. But the stone-hearted child of King Bimbisara had me thrown out, with a stern warning that I would be beheaded if I were caught again.

My only refuge now was at Venuvana. The *bhikkhus* understood my pain and offered silent commiseration. An old friend in the Palace guard informed us that King Bimbisara bore his situation with equanimity. He spent a considerable amount of time in meditation, he said. Then he would sit by his window, looking out towards Vulture peak. Despite his rapidly deteriorating health, his spirits did not flag and he greeted his guards cheerfully every morning.

Queen Videhi was distraught and sought the Buddha's counsel. He sent a young *bhikkhu* to Kosala, to request King Pasenadi's intervention in this grave crisis. Little did we know that the Buddha himself would be the next target.

The Buddha's days were normally spent in meeting the many lay people who came to him for guidance. Learned men came to find out more about his teachings. The *bhikkhus* would be enthralled by these debates, for they cleared many of their own doubts. But no matter how long and busy his day, the Buddha would meditate deep into the night. The *bhikkhus* reported that he slept for only three or four hours every day.

One night, though, he had visitors. Armed ones. Sensing their presence, he opened his eyes and called out to them gently, in his calm, compassionate voice. The men dropped their weapons and approaching the Master, fell at his feet, weeping in regret.

"Lord, we were supposed to kill you. But we are unable to even lift the bows or draw the swords! Please forgive us and accept us as your disciples!"

Next morning, the news of this attempt on the Buddha's life and the presence of the new disciples caused great excitement and agitation at Venuvana.

Hurtling boulder

Shriranga and I were returning from making our food offering to the *bhikkhus*. We had spent the afternoon listening to a talk given by Venerable Ananda to the young *bhikkhus*. He was the younger brother of the wretched Devadatta and we marvelled at his sweet and gentle temperament. He was a devoted attendant of the Buddha and it was said he had done his best to stop Devadatta from breaking up the Sangha.

The sun was setting as we were leaving Venuvana. It was then that we heard that yet another attempt had been made on the Buddha's life. This time a huge boulder had been hurled down the mountain slope as the Buddha stood by his hut on Vulture Peak, enjoying the sunset. Fortunately, the boulder had crashed into two huge rocks and burst into a thousand fragments. One shard had injured the Buddha's foot, though.

We rushed to Vulture Peak. The *bhikkhus* were trying to get a stretcher and some bandages, for the Master's foot was bleeding profusely. We joined a band that combed the hillside, looking for the culprits. These two attempts on the Buddha's life were causing great concern among the *bhikkhus* who now decided that there must be a guard formed within the Sangha to protect the Master.

But the Buddha would hear none of it, admonishing all of us instead, "There is no need for all this noise and commotion. I don't need protection, I am safe on Vulture Peak." he said. But he did allow me to fetch Jivaka and have his bleeding foot attended to.

A few days later, we heard that King Bimbisara had passed away. He was found lying by his window, eyes open, gazing out towards Vulture Peak.

Raging elephant

One day, the Buddha was in the capital, begging for his meal with other *bhikkhus*. Suddenly, there was pandemonium. People were fleeing in panic, some even climbing up to safer heights, for the elephant Nalagiri was on the rampage. It had somehow escaped from its stables and was stomping through the town, crushing anything that stood in its path.

Many of the *bhikkhus* ran away. Venerable Ananda tried to drag the Buddha to safety, but the Master stood firm. As the elephant charged towards them, Venerable Ananda stepped in its path, to stop it from hurting the Buddha. But it was not just human beings who were overcome in the presence of the Exalted One. The elephant that just moments ago had been drunk with rage, stopped in his tracks and knelt down in front of the Buddha. He extended his trunk like a baby seeking a loving caress. The Buddha spoke soft words and stroked him gently. And the elephant drew great, shuddering breaths as it tuned into life's rhythm once again.

Meanwhile, Venerable Sariputta and Venerable Moggallana had decided to spend a few days with the breakaway Sangha. The foolish Devadatta gleefully announced that they, too, had left the Buddha's group to join him. He permitted Venerable Sariputta to guide the *bhikkhus* in his group, for he was aware of the formidable depth of Sariputta's wisdom.

One day, sensing an opportunity, Venerable Sariputta announced that he was going back to the Buddha and asked if any of the *bhikkhus* would like to join him. By now the *bhikkhus* had realised what they had lost by leaving the Buddha. Close to 450 of them returned to the Buddha's fold. They were welcomed back like long-lost brothers.

REFUGE IN THE DHAMMA

Ajatasattu did not grieve King Bimbisara's death, but King Pasenadi certainly did. He decided to avenge the death of his brother-in-law. When King Bimbisara had married Queen Videhi, she had been gifted a large territory in dowry. This was a fertile piece of land and generated substantial revenues for the kingdom. We heard that King Pasenadi had insisted that the territory be returned to Kosala.

Ajatasattu waged a war in defence of that territory. It was a long and terrible battle that lasted over six months. Ajatasattu attacked with all the might of the Magadhan army. Heavy artillery pounded the borders of the Kosala kingdom. One day, we heard that victory was just moments away. But King Pasenadi's forces regrouped and they pitched battle again. This time, Magadha's army was routed and the King, along with his commanders, was taken captive. What next, we wondered, for the tradition of warrior kings demanded a complete humiliation of the vanquished.

King Pasenadi sought the Buddha's counsel; and the Master said to him:

"Treat him with all the respect due to a King. Guide him with the love you have in your heart for your nephew and he will receive it well. Whatever you do now will be a true test of your skills at governance as well as your progress on the path of Dhamma."

The King went back immersed in thought, and a couple of days later announced that he was releasing King Ajatasattu from captivity with full honour. He also announced that he was returning the disputed property to Magadha. There was more to follow – the King was also giving his daughter in marriage to Ajatasattu!

It was a rather subdued King Ajatasattu who returned to the throne of Magadha. As the days passed, remorse crept softly into his wicked heart. He was tormented and distraught, and could not perform his duties. Finally, Jivaka prevailed upon him to turn to the Buddha for guidance.

"The Buddha? He must hate me for what I have done. He was my Father's teacher. How can I go to him?"

But Jivaka explained to him that the Buddha's compassion knew no bounds. And Ajatasattu sought relief from suffering in the wisdom and liberating teachings of the Buddha.

Venerable Devadatta too experienced sorrow and regret, as he grew older. He decided to come back to the Buddha's fold. On his way, however, he was taken seriously ill, and had to be carried in to the Buddha's hut. Chanting the three refuges, he passed away at the Master's feet.

One cool spring evening, I set off for a walk and found myself climbing up to the Buddha's hut on Vulture Peak. He was in Savatthi and I sat outside, all alone. So many years had passed since King Bimbisara and I had first set eyes on the young monk Siddhartha. So many lives had since been touched and transformed. And though the countryside that stretched below was the same as before, one man's Awakening had enabled a simple charioteer to understand that he was but a spot of colour in this beautiful mural of life.

Book III: Ananda
Attendant of the Buddha

CARING FOR THE MASTER

The Buddha was 55 year old when he expressed exhaustion with his duties for the first time. He had been travelling and teaching for 20 years now and it was only during the monsoon retreat that he stayed in one location for three months. Otherwise, he was on the move every two to three days.

Many people other than disciples also sought his counsel everyday – lay people, ascetics, kings, courtiers, Brahmins, even beggars and courtesans. He asked Sariputta to find one among the monks who could serve as his personal attendant and help him cope with these tasks.

The Sangha had grown over the years; no one had realised that continuous travel and rigorous discipline were taking their toll on the Master. Sariputta immediately offered to serve him himself. But the Buddha refused to accept, saying,

"When you are at a monastery, I need not go there, Sariputta! You have rendered me great service already, by realising and spreading the message of the Great Way. The *bhikkhus* need your guidance, the Sangha needs your supervision."

Kondanna, Moggallana, Mahakassapa and many other senior monks offered too. But he refused each one. Only I sat silent.

Sariputta then summoned a meeting that evening and announced to the assembly:

"The Master needs an attendant, *bhikkhus*! Someone who can assist him with his visitors, who can fetch him some water when he is thirsty and who will shake the creases out of his sheet at night with loving care."

We sat in silent contemplation. And then I heard my name being recommended!

"Ananda should be appointed to care for the Master. He is sincere and devoted. He is also young enough to cope with his own tasks and tend to the Master's needs," said one.

"Besides, he has a great memory! He will be present at all the Master's meetings and can repeat for us everything the Master speaks – whether at discourses or as advice to those who come to meet him," said another.

And the *bhikkhus* nodded in agreement.

"Ananda is the ideal choice," they said. But I refused to even consider the idea.

"To serve as the Master's personal attendant is an honour and, indeed, a rare privilege! But I cannot accept it, Venerable Sariputta! Many may consider this a favour I have been granted, for I am a cousin of the Exalted One. Any merit I acquire will be construed as special favours bestowed upon me by the Master. Oh no, no! I cannot accept this post, Venerables! For I know only too well how firm the Buddha is about these issues. Young *bhikkhus* learn very early on that Rahula is the son of my cousin. But it is months before they realise who this cousin is, who Rahula's father is!"

Sariputta persisted. "We know you are incapable of petty action, Ananda! Why must you hold back from doing what is right and honourable by your Master, merely for fear that some may misunderstand? Think of how much the Sangha will benefit by your being appointed attendant to the Buddha. We need your assistance to preserve the Master's wisdom, Ananda! Step forward and perform your duty!"

Finally, I agreed. But I had many conditions! The Master would never offer me any of his robes nor would he share his food offering with me, I insisted. I would never dwell in the same hut with him and another *bhikkhu* would accompany us, if he and I were invited to a lay disciple's house for a meal offering. He must permit me to exercise discretion in admitting visitors into his presence, I said firmly. And he would always accompany me when I visited a lay person's house to receive alms. He would clarify any doubts on the Dhamma that I may have, from time to time and finally, he would repeat to me any discourse or advice he had given when I was not present.

The Buddha was informed about the choice and about the conditions it came with. "Ananda will do just fine!" he said and accepted me as his attendant.

I treasured the opportunity I now had of serving the Master. With time, I was able to anticipate and fulfil his needs before he even expressed them. I learned how to manage his visitors, so that none went away disappointed, while still making sure that my Master was not weary at the end of the day. When he rested at night, I walked around his hut nine times with a lit torch, to make sure he rested well.

As I stayed close to him, I saw what a frugal, simple life he led. Waking up well before dawn, he would bathe and sit in meditation for a long while. Later, when the sun was high, he would go on his alms round, sometimes alone but often accompanied by a few of us. It was from him that I learnt how to seek alms. He would stand silently before a dwelling, eyes downcast, his bowl held aloft with infinite grace. If no alms were offered, he moved on quietly. When some food was received, he bowed in deepest humility, offering the soft words of his teaching in gratitude.

Sometimes, we would be invited into the home and they would offer us a portion of their own meal, hot and freshly cooked. But it was not unusual to receive rancid leftovers. We accepted both with neither clinging nor aversion, as he had taught us. Jivaka, the physician, cautioned us, however. All foods did not stay well overnight, he told us, consuming them makes you ill; so we would place the rancid offerings into the earth.

A large part of the Master's day was spent in guiding his disciples. He watched over his flock, never once expressing impatience or irritation. Depending on the level of awareness achieved by each one, he offered suggestions and kind words of encouragement. He would meet lay disciples and other visitors in the evening. I don't believe I ever saw him at a loss for an answer, even though many intellectuals came armed with clever questions to trip him up! Everywhere, he left behind people transformed from just having met him once, from having heard him speak just that one time under the tree in the village square.

Once we were in Kesaputta, the village where the Kalama tribe dwelled. And they said to him,

"Master, we have heard many wonderful stories of your wisdom. Pray, help us resolve a grave issue that confronts us. Many ascetics and learned Brahmins preach to us various doctrines of salvation. Each proclaims the superiority of his own teaching. How are we simple folk to judge which teaching is truly meaningful and which is to be discarded as false and ill-conceived?"

And the Wise One spoke to the Kalamas:

"You have done well to raise this question! Do not believe in a doctrine merely because someone says so, or because it is written in the scriptures or because it is taught by one who is venerated by all. Accept only that which is in accord with your own reason. Observe only those practices that bring forth the wholesome states of equanimity and quiet joy. Such practices have the support of the wise and the virtuous.

When you find a doctrine that is not in accord with your reason, you will do well to discard it immediately as one that is ill-conceived. If the practices you are asked to observe by such a teacher do not lead to states of equanimity and quiet joy, know that such a teaching cannot have the support of the wise and the virtuous."

And the Kalamas were delighted to find a Teacher who did not demand blind faith.

"Such a one is truly fearless," they said, and many asked to be accepted as his disciples.

TALES OF THE SANGHA

My duties as attendant to the Master filled my day. I did get some time to myself, though not very often. Then, the younger monks would seek me out, for many of them experienced difficulties. Most were prepared for the humble living but sitting for meditation was a great struggle. Legs ached and the mind wandered. Many shed tears of frustration. But they settled down with time. Every now and then, they would ask about the Master and how some of his disciples came to join the Sangha. And I was happy to oblige, for story-telling has always served to inspire and create a sense of belonging among people. We would sit together in my hut and wander back in time to the early days of the Sangha...

Sakya Nobles Join the Sangha

Cousin Aniruddha had been deeply moved by the Buddha when he visited Kapilavatthu after attaining Enlightenment. One evening, he spoke to all of us,

"Look upon Siddhartha now. He knows no anger, no hatred, no fear. He is serene and radiant with the most profound love for all beings – should we also not follow the Path that leads to this Awakening?"

And so, Aniruddha, Bhaddiya, Devadatta, Bhagu, Kimbila and myself set off one day to join the Sangha. We met Upali, the barber, on the way.

"Shave our heads, Upali," we said to him. And when he was done, we gave him our fine clothes and jewellery.

"We are going to become monks and we have no use for all this," we said to the shocked fellow. "Make yourself a good life with this wealth!"

We proceeded towards Malla, where the Buddha was dwelling at that time. Soon, however, Upali caught up with us, gasping for breath. And he was not carrying any of the finery we had given him. Had bandits made off with his booty?

"No, kind sirs! After you left, I looked at the precious jewels you gave me and my heart was filled with great joy! I will be able to live in luxury all my life, I thought. But then I realised that no one would believe me, if I said this wealth had been donated to me. They would suspect me of waylaying an innocent prince!

And I began to wonder why such young, robust noblemen would leave the comfort and luxury of their palaces to pursue the lives of monks. I had heard the Buddha speak in Nigrodha Park when he returned to Kapilavatthu. I had heard him say that greed led to unhappiness and sorrow of the deepest magnitude. I did not want to be trapped by all that wealth, so I hung the bundle on a tree for a good soul to find. I want to go to the Buddha too, please take me along! I have rushed as fast as I could to catch up with you, sires!"

We were amazed by the barber and we let him accompany us. When we reached Malla, the Buddha asked us who it was that was trailing behind us – it was Upali the barber, we told him and narrated his story.

The Buddha asked him to come forward to be ordained first. We protested that he was only a barber and he should wait until we were ordained. But the Master's voice rang out:

"You seek the Path to Liberation still clinging to narrow ideas of caste and birth! You should know that the Sangha makes no distinction amongst people. Merit is acquired through diligent practice and the Way is for all to walk, with equality and freedom!"

And so, Upali was ordained before the rest of us. I took the vows of a novice monk, as I was just 18 at the time.

I faced many hurdles in my practice. I was soft hearted and I could not cut clean through the vines of delusion that sprang up and entangled me, every time my vigil slackened. I also had more than my fair share of trouble with women – foremost amongst them was the Matanga girl from whom I asked a drink of water.

I was out begging on a hot summer's day and I was extremely thirsty. A young girl was drawing water at a well and I asked her if I could have some. But she was overcome with terror and begged me to leave. "Please, O Venerable Sir, do not speak to me, go away! We lowborn ones are not permitted to offer you water. I will be cursed forever, should you even step into my shadow!"

"It is a hot day and I am thirsty. Please, all I want is some water!" I persisted.

But her whole frame shook with agitation. I told her the Buddha's teachings did not differentiate between people.

"You are a human being, just like me! So please, can I have some water?"

She glowed with joy at these words and stepped forward to pour some water into my cupped hands. After that day, I noticed she was always at the well when I went begging. She would offer me water, even if I did not ask. I smiled at her with all the compassion in my heart and she seemed to blossom in happiness each day. Twice I accepted a meal offering at her house. But then, the hot flush on her face alerted me and I refused to go again.

One day she pleaded that her mother wished to make just one more meal offering. I hesitated, but she pressed on. Not wanting to hurt her feelings, I went to their dwelling. I detected the poison in the very first morsel. I began observing my breath, sitting still, eyes closed. Mother and daughter whispered in puzzlement, but I did not move.

How long I sat, I do not know. But when I heard the anxious voices of some *bhikkhus* calling out for me, I gratefully rushed up to meet them. I told them what had happened. They took mother and daughter along with me to the Buddha.

The mother confessed. She said she had tried to explain to the girl the impossibility of her situation.

"But she would neither rest nor eat, consumed as she was by her love for the monk Ananda! Finally, I decided to help her out of her misery. I made a mixture of some intoxicants and mixed it in his food! I beg your pardon, most humbly, Venerable Ananda, for trying to break your vows! But I could not bear to see my child in such distress!"

The Master discussed the episode that evening and asked the *bhikkhus* to practise mindfulness at all times, to avoid getting trapped in such situations. Never had I imagined that a monk's life would be so fraught with peril! We left the meeting hall in thoughtful silence.

Or so I thought! The *bhikkhus* could not wait to get around the corner, out of the Master's earshot. They howled with laughter at my latest escapade!

"What is it with you and women, Ananda? They find you irresistible, even in a monk's garb!"

My ears burned and I walked away hastily, plagued with a sense of my own weakness. There were many women among the lay disciples and we were often required to instruct them on the Dhamma. I had to make sure these situations did not recur, so I decided to seek the Master's help. I went to his hut and found him preparing to rest for the night. Helping him lay the sheet on the floor, I asked him:

"Master, pray tell me, how do we conduct ourselves with respect to women?"
"Do not look upon them, Ananda!"
"But if we see them, then what must we do?"

"Do not speak to them, Ananda!"

"But Master, what if they speak to us? What, then, must a *bhikkhu* do?"

"Keep wide awake, Ananda!"

And he lay down and closed his eyes. I crept away, but not before checking again to see if he was really asleep. For I had a feeling Siddhartha, too, was laughing at me that night!

Bhikkhuni Gotami

The entry of women into the Sangha had not been easy. Had it not been for the strong will of the Master's foster mother, they would never have been permitted to take the vows of *bhikkhunis*.

We were at Vesali when I saw the strange sight outside the monastery gates – a large group of women, in orange robes, with shorn heads and swollen, bleeding feet. I stared at their leader – could this be Mother Gotami?

"Yes, Ananda," she said, tearfully.

After the passing of King Shuddhodana, Mother Gotami had asked to be ordained in the Sangha. But the Buddha had refused, saying the Sangha was not yet ready to accept women into its fold. But Mother Gotami was a determined lady. She persuaded many noblewomen to join her. And they set off from Kapilavatthu, walking barefoot, begging bowls in hand. Citizens of Magadha lined the streets, overcome with emotion at the sight of these noble ladies, in humble robes, seeking the Way of the Enlightened One.

"Mother Gotami, please turn back! The Way is long and hard, you are too tender to bear its rigours!" they pleaded.

But the women walked on, braving forests and overflowing streams, to arrive tearstained and exhausted in Vesali. They just had to show the Buddha that they were not afraid of monastic life.

I rushed to the Buddha's hut and told him what I'd seen. I entreated him to allow them in. But he refused. Three times I requested and three times he refused.

Finally I asked him, "Master, if women observe the discipline of a *bhikkhu's* life and practice meditation to walk on the Path of Dhamma, can they too attain Nirvana?"

"All beings are capable of attaining the fruits of practice, Ananda," he replied.

Then I could not hold back.

"Master, Mother Gotami nursed you as a new-born, after your own mother passed away. She has never caused anyone to doubt the depth of her love and devotion to you. After your visit to Kapilavatthu, she has diligently practised the precepts for lay disciples and ever followed the teachings of the Great Way to Liberation. Mother Gotami now stands outside the monastery gates, having walked twenty days from Kapilavatthu in bare feet and with no possessions save a begging bowl. What more do you want them to do? If, as you say, there is no difference between what men and women can achieve on this Path, please, I beseech you, let them be ordained!"

And to my utter surprise, he agreed!

But he was concerned about the harmony within the Sangha as well as opposition from lay disciples. Special rules were laid down for the women to observe strictly, if they wanted to join the Order. They had to submit to the seniority of a *bhikkhu*, no matter how recently he may have joined the Sangha. They could not criticise a *bhikkhu* and were not permitted to ever give Dhamma instruction to them. They had to complete two years as novices, before being fully ordained. They had to seek the guidance of *bhikkhus* twice a month and confess any transgressions in front of the *bhikkhunis* as well as the *bhikkhus*. They had to spend the retreat season near a centre for *bhikkhus* and report their progress to both, *bhikkhunis* and *bhikkhus*.

Mother Gotami was not disheartened by these stringent rules. The women wanted to follow in the footsteps of the Buddha – all else was a matter of detail. In the years to come, Princess Yashodhara too took the vows of a *bhikkhuni*. She was an able assistant to Bhikkhuni Gotami in organising the women into the fold of the Sangha.

Many *bhikkhunis* excelled in their grasp of the Dhamma and gave fine discourses on the Master's teachings. Once, when a lay disciple reported the exquisite elaboration of Bhikkhuni Dhammadinna on the Noble Eightfold Path, the Master asked

me to remember everything she had said and repeat it to the
bhikkhus that evening.

The Dispute at Kosambi

I was watching dust dance in the path of light. It was dawn
and I was waiting by the Buddha's hut, as I had waited every
morning for months, hoping he would return. It was a year
and four months since that terrible day at Gosita's monastery
and I could not bear the thought of not seeing the Master
again. I wished the quarrel had never broken out.

It was the ninth monsoon retreat after the Master's
Enlightenment. We were spending it in the forest that lay
disciple Gosita had donated, outside the city of Kosambi. A
bhikkhu had been accused of not observing a precept and
some of the others announced his expulsion.

Now this *bhikkhu* had studied the Dhamma well. He
presented many arguments in his defence, refusing to accept
that he had done anything wrong. But the others were firm
in their opinion. Soon, the *bhikkhus* were divided – one group
insisting on the strict observance of the Rules and the other
advocating their interpretation in the spirit of the Dhamma.
As the days passed, tempers flared and harsh words, as yet
unspoken in the monastery, were being flung to and fro.

The Buddha spoke separately to each group, asking them
not to stick rigidly to their own positions. But they were in
the grip of madness and they continued slandering and reviling

103

each other. Finally, a meeting of all *bhikkhus* in the monastery was summoned. And the Blessed One addressed them, saying:

"Disputes and strife reign in the world outside the monastery walls. How can anyone have faith in the Dhamma when we do the same things, in spite of our vows and practice? This ceaseless arguing will only create a rift in the Sangha. Desist from this divisive behaviour, *bhikkhus*! We practice the Way to quell the fires of hatred and intolerance!"

A young *bhikkhu* rose to his feet and announced:

"Master, why do you bother with our quarrel? You should dwell peacefully in your meditation. Go back to your practice! We can sort this matter out ourselves!"

In the stunned silence that followed, the Buddha picked up his begging bowl and walked out of the monastery. Days passed, but he did not return. And yet the quarrelsome fools kept arguing!

Lay disciples were alarmed and disturbed by this behaviour. They had looked forward to the retreat, for they treasured the opportunity for personal guidance from the Blessed One. They spoke to the warring *bhikkhus* and asked them to follow the Teaching and end the quarrel. But the *bhikkhus* paid no attention. Finally, the lay disciples refused to make any more food offerings to them, saying,

"You are not worthy of wearing the orange robes of the Sangha. People have lost faith in you. Only if you make a confession to the Master can you regain our respect and trust," they said to the *bhikkhus*. Fearing the pangs of hunger, the *bhikkhus* agreed to meet and resolve the conflict.

I looked for the Master in the forests around Kosambi, but he was nowhere to be found. I travelled to Savatthi, but he was not at the Jetavana monastery either. Sariputta, Moggallana, Devadatta, Kimbila, Mahakassapa and many other senior disciples were there, along with Bhikkhuni Gotami and young Rahula. They comforted me. Sariputta was convinced the Master would never abandon us.

And so I waited at Jetavana, keeping his hut ready for his return. I had finished sweeping it out when, through the haze of dust and misery, a familiar figure shimmered into view. And a dear, familiar voice spoke:

"Ah, there you are Ananda!"

"Master! Where have you been? How I have longed for just one glimpse of you!" I rushed outside and plucked a small bunch of wild flowers to offer him in welcome. He accepted them graciously but dismissed me brusquely:

"Ananda! Do not spend your time in adoring and worshipping the Buddha! You serve the Master best by practising the Way to gain true Understanding!"

This was what had drawn us to the Sangha, this clear, ringing voice that wasted not one breath. To sit at his feet was to experience all the wonders of this life. He had wrought human qualities to a perfection so fine, that the mantle of purity sat light on his shoulders. He had extinguished all flames of desire, his intense stillness containing the power of thunderbolts.

He sat down as if he had never been away. As the *bhikkhus* gathered to welcome him, he enquired after their practice and answered their queries. I stood by, with Sariputta, unwilling to take my eyes off him, in case he disappeared again. He asked about the quarrelsome *bhikkhus* of Kosambi. He sat with Sariputta awhile, discussing the need to ensure harmony within the Sangha, as it attracted more and more disciples from diverse backgrounds.

A few days later, we heard that the *bhikkhus* from Kosambi were on their way to Savatthi, to make a confession to the Master. Sariputta asked how they should be dealt with. And the Blessed One said:

"Do not recriminate or speak harsh words, Sariputta, for that will only make them more obstinate about their views. Welcome them warmly and give them separate dwellings for some time. Let both sides present their views. And remember, the action which is onward leading, which promotes peace and harmony, that is the action in accordance with the Dhamma. Guide them to a genuine reconciliation, Sariputta! Discord within the Sangha discourages lay people from embracing the Teaching."

By that evening, each side had sought the forgiveness of the other. After the confession ceremony, some of us sat together late that night. We marvelled at the Master's conduct throughout this unhappy episode. And Aniruddha, always the contemplative observer, said to all of us:

"We are fortunate in having the Blessed One as the Master. When confronted by doubt and failure, we need to only dwell upon him, for he embodies the Teaching. He has the compassion to lead us on, no matter in what shape we arrive. Look around this monastery. Some *bhikkhus* are unable to recite even one *sutra* of the Master's teaching, yet they make progress on this Path. About them he says:

"It is not important to know and recite the *sutras*, it is important to live the knowledge."

Then there are *bhikkhus* who are weak in the body, yet they force themselves through long hours of practice. To them he says:

"Do not exert beyond the limits of your ability. This body needs to be fit and healthy to realise the fruits of practice. If you are constantly fatigued, you will soon be overcome by disappointment."

But should you be revelling in laziness, then it was a different story! As it was for me, when we joined the Sangha. I was used to soft linen and delicious meals in Kapilavatthu. The way of the Sangha was hard and wearying. One day, during the Master's discourse, I fell asleep! He called me aside and asked:

'Aniruddha, did you take the vows of a monk to escape from your responsibilities as a royal?'
'No, Master, I seek the Way out of the suffering of old age, disease and death, I seek the Way as taught by Sakyamuni, the Buddha!'

'And do you think by dozing in your Master's presence, you will acquire this knowledge?' He had shamed me out of my lethargy!

The Master crafts the Way so that all can walk upon it, with their inherent abilities and weaknesses."

I was grateful to Aniruddha for his insight.

Sariputta and Moggallana: Jewels of the Sangha

Sariputta and Moggallana had been friends from childhood. Both were blessed with formidable intellectual ability and had great respect for each other. They enrolled as students of Sanjaya, the sceptic, and soon became his foremost disciples. But they longed for a teacher who would lead them to the elusive goal of Enlightenment and they knew it was not Sanjaya. They promised each other that should either of them find one such, he would tell the other.

One day, Sariputta was walking in Rajagaha and he chanced upon a monk begging for food. The monk walked with calm, measured steps, eyes downcast, his whole being radiating peace and tranquillity. Sariputta was struck by his appearance and followed the monk. He waited till the monk had finished his begging round and eaten his meal. Presenting himself, he enquired about the monk and his teacher.

The monk replied, "I am Assaji and I study the Doctrine of Enlightenment as taught by Sakyamuni."

"And what is the Doctrine this Master teaches?" asked Sariputta, trembling with excitement.

"I cannot tell you much, as I have joined his Sangha only recently. But I can tell you briefly," Assaji replied. And he proceeded to recite a *gatha*:

"Whatever from a cause proceeds, thereof
the Tathagata has explained the cause.
Its cessation too he has explained.
This is the teaching of the Supreme Sage."

As he heard Assaji, Sariputta attained a deep insight into the Way of Enlightenment and he rushed back to Moggallana to narrate the meeting with the monk. They both decided this was the Master they would follow and they went to meet the Buddha in the Bamboo Grove.

On meeting the two friends, the Buddha said, "These two will become the jewels of the Sangha."

Sariputta attained Enlightenment about a year later, at the age of 28. He had grasped the profound depths of his Master's teaching and was able to expound them in simple terms to young disciples. And he remained forever compassionate and humble, quietly cleaning up after the *bhikkhus* when they went on their begging rounds. It was to his care that the Master entrusted his own son, Rahula.

As the Sangha grew in numbers, it was critical to ensure that the *bhikkhus* did not burden the lay community with their requirements of food, robes and medicine. It was

Sariputta's skills at organisation and leadership that were responsible for the orderly movement of *bhikkhus* from one location to another, for their living arrangements and provisions for food.

Once, when he was at Savatthi, supervising the building of the Jetavana monastery with Sudatta, he met a monk whom he knew from earlier times. When the monk learned that Sariputta was a disciple of the Buddha, he raised his eyebrows in surprise:

"Oh, you still need a teacher? I abandoned all Masters long ago. I now seek my own path!"

Sariputta replied, "A calf abandons the milk of a frenzied cow, after just wetting its lips. Your Master must not have attained Enlightenment, which is why you left him. Just as one can never tire of the nourishing milk of a healthy cow, so too can I never grow weary of my Master's teachings – they are inexhaustible."

As for Moggallana, he was deeply committed to attaining the wisdom taught by his Master. He retired to Vulture Peak to practice and would hardly sleep or rest. His faith and devotion for the Buddha were legendary. They said he heard the soft voice of the Buddha constantly through his meditations. Whenever he was discouraged, the Buddha would appear before him with words of encouragement, exhorting him to persevere.

As the teachings of the Buddha spread through the region, many youth joined the Sangha. Many kings and nobles supported the Sangha and helped establish the monasteries that are now great centres for retreat and study. However, this gave rise to feelings of jealousy and rivalry among other religious groups. Moggallana was a blunt and outspoken person. Whenever there was a debate about prevailing religious belief in the light of the Buddha's teaching, he spoke eloquently and without hesitation about his Master's teachings. He was often the object of persecution, as people felt slighted by his vigorous defence of the Buddha's teachings.

Mahakassapa

Mahakassapa was born into an extremely wealthy Brahmin family. They had 25 storerooms filled with gold, silver and other valuable articles; they had more land under cultivation than the King himself.

But from an early age, Mahakassapa showed an inclination for monastic life. His parents were worried and constantly entreated him to get married and gift them the joy of becoming grandparents. Mahakassapa resisted their entreaties as long as he could. Then, to stop them altogether, he fashioned a sculpture of a woman in pure gold. She was so incredibly beautiful as to be unreal. "If you can find a girl who looks like this, I will marry her," he declared, confident that it would never happen.

However, his parents searched the entire kingdom and neighbouring lands as well – and found a young girl who matched the statue of gold in every respect! Bound by his word, Mahakassapa married her. But his views influenced his wife and she too began to tread the path leading to monastic life. Alas, the old parents died without a grandchild.

Mahakassapa donned the mantle of the head of the family in order to look after the family's vast fortune. One day, though, he had an insight that changed his life forever. He was watching farm labourers till the soil. As they ploughed through the soft earth, he saw millions of tiny insects being churned up and killed under the hoe. As he watched, he understood the impermanent nature of life and decided then and there that he would become a monk. His wife understood him completely and did not stop him.

When he was near Nalanda, not far from Rajagaha, Mahakassapa saw the Buddha resting under a tree. He was struck by the compassion and serenity of the Buddha's countenance.

"This is my teacher," he exclaimed softly to himself.

He fell at the Buddha's feet and asked to be accepted as a disciple. The Buddha agreed; in gratitude, Mahakassapa folded his robe and invited the Buddha to sit on it. When the Buddha remarked how soft the robe was, Mahakassapa insisted on the Master accepting his robe as a gift. The Buddha gave him his own in exchange and Mahakassapa treasured it all his life.

For a man who had lived in opulent luxury, Mahakassapa adopted the ascetic life of the monks with ease. In fact, when the members of the Sangha began receiving soft, well-made robes from laity, Mahakassapa continued to wear his rough robes of rags stitched together.

He was often the butt of jokes amongst the young monks for his strange appearance. One day, the Buddha invited him to sit next to him and announced, "Mahakassapa's ascetic ways are in no way different from my own practices." And they smirked at him no more.

As they aged however, the Buddha became concerned about Mahakassapa's health. He suggested that Mahakassapa could sleep in a hut now and not insist on sleeping under trees.

"It is alright to accept some of the robes and food the wealthy offer – you do not have to beg every day."

Mahakassapa was taken aback and replied,

"Master, I still have the robe you gave me and I have preserved it with honour and gratitude. I have never found asceticism a difficult discipline to follow – in fact, it brings me great joy. It helps me keep alive the attitude I had when I first joined the Sangha. And Master, I have found plenty in just sufficiency!"

"You have spoken well," said the Great Master. And Mahakassapa continued to lead a simple life.

Angulimala

The Buddha had been meditating in Jetavana. One day, he entered a village on the outskirts of Savatthi to beg. He was surprised to find a ghost town, all doors and windows tightly shut and not even an animal in sight. He waited in front of a house with his bowl, in case there was someone there. The door creaked open and a pair of eyes peeped out. Suddenly, it opened wider and he was pulled inside.

"What are you doing in the open? Don't you know Angulimala has been spotted outside the village last night?" they asked him.

The Buddha asked who this Angulimala was and why everyone was so afraid.

"He is a fearsome murderer! Whenever he kills someone, he cuts off a finger and wears it around his neck. He says he wants a hundred fingers for his necklace, then he will gain some more evil powers! That is why he is called Angulimala! You better have your meal indoors today, Master!"

But the Buddha refused. "If people are to have faith in my teaching, I must walk," he thought.

And he continued down the street with his slow, meditative step. Soon, he heard footsteps behind him. He continued walking, knowing fully well it was Angulimala.

"Stop, stop!" the man called out. The Buddha merely continued on his way, neither hurrying nor panicking.

"Stop monk, if you value your life, STOP!" Angulimala cried again. But the Fearless One would not stop. Finally, he caught up with the Buddha and stood in front of him.

"Why didn't you stop when I told you to? Don't you know who I am?"

"I know you, Angulimala!" said the Buddha, gazing deep into those frenzied eyes with love and compassion. No one had ever looked on with such tenderness at the murderer before. Tears welled up in his eyes and he dropped down on his knees.

"Help me, Master! I have been leading a life of delusion. I have committed such horrible crimes that it is not possible for me to return to normal life now."

"It is never too late, Angulimala. Stop travelling this road of hatred and violence. I will protect you, if you take the vows of a *bhikkhu* and devote your time to practising the Way."

Angulimala sobbed uncontrollably. The Master led him to Jetavana. He was given a robe and Sariputta shaved his head. He then knelt and recited the three refuges.

Angulimala turned out to be one of the most sincere *bhikkhus* ever to join the Sangha. In a short while, he acquired the glow that comes only from devoted practice. He was renamed 'Ahimsaka' – meaning the non-violent one. Many months later, the *bhikkhus* were witness to an event that showed just how much Ahimsaka had advanced on the Path of Dhamma.

115

Ahimsaka had been to a village on his alms round, when some people recognised him as the murderer Angulimala. They began pelting him with stones and beating him with sticks. Ahimsaka did not strike them back nor did he try to stop them. He merely cowered down, his palms joined together in a prayerful gesture. They beat him up mercilessly, stopping only when he began to vomit blood.

Somehow he managed to drag himself back to the grove where the rest of the *bhikkhus* were dwelling, his robe torn and his begging bowl shattered. Though he was severely wounded he did not cry out. There was tremendous concern at his condition and the Buddha arrived to comfort him. On hearing his tale, the Buddha said:

"Ananda, get a poultice for his wounds. Enduring the pain of these wounds will wash away the pain of your past, Ahimsaka. You did well to not retaliate."

Ahimsaka had truly become a model of non-violence in the Sangha.

Sunita

Sunita was an Untouchable. He had grown up in the segregated dwellings of the low caste people. He knew he would be cursed forever if he drew water from a well meant for the upper castes. He took great care when he walked, making sure his shadow did not fall upon anyone, compelling them to bathe again and perform purification rites.

One day, Sunita was clearing night soil by the riverbank, when he saw the Buddha approaching on the road. He stepped aside, so that his shadow would not defile such a great master. The Buddha changed his direction and started walking towards Sunita. Poor Sunita scampered hither and thither, like a cornered mouse, to get out of the Buddha's way. He found himself walking backwards down the riverbank and still the Buddha relentlessly continued to approach him. The poor man was now in the river, standing waist deep in water. He could not retreat any further.

The Buddha then spoke compassionately to Sunita and asked him if he would like an opportunity to live a life of a *bhikkhu*, with no barriers between him and other beings.

"How is that possible?" cried Sunita. He was sure he would be beaten up for this transgression – first of standing so close to the Buddha and then for even speaking to him.

But the Buddha led him gently out of the water and offered him a dry robe. He explained to him that his followers believed in the equality of all beings. They were respected as persons of learning and they practised the Way diligently, so as to attain Liberation in their lifetime.

Sunita chose to join the Sangha.

The Buddha then bathed him, with Sariputta's help. Sunita chanted the three refuges there, by the riverbank, and went to dwell in Jetavana. He was a sincere *bhikkhu*. So diligently did he practice that he made rapid progress on the Path and he was soon given charge of young novice monks.

But the inclusion of an Untouchable in the Sangha caused a furore amongst the citizens of Kosala. King Pasenadi's advisors objected very strongly.

"This is inexcusable, Your Majesty! An Untouchable has been ordained in the Sangha! We have been very accommodating so far, no matter that the Buddha continually challenges our practices and traditions. But this act cannot be condoned. You must protest, Your Majesty!"

The King, although fairly liberal in his views, was also convinced that this time the Buddha was carrying things too far. He asked for his carriage and left for Jetavana at once.

As he walked through the grove on his way to the Buddha's hut, he passed a group of young novices listening intently to a young *bhikkhu's* discourse on the Buddha's teachings. So well had the *bhikkhu* imbibed the essence of the Buddha's message that even the King halted and listened to him awhile. Then, recalling the purpose of his mission, he carried on towards the Buddha's dwelling.

The Buddha heard him out and said, "Your Majesty, for too long have we judged people according to the circumstances of their birth. Sunita bleeds when his skin is cut. His blood is thick and red, just as yours is, Your Majesty. His tears taste of salt, just as ours do. When we treat people as Untouchables, we cause them grave injury. We create divisions where none need exist. Considering that we are made of the same elements, we must extend the liberating knowledge of this Path to all beings."

The King was not sure what to say. He could understand the Buddha's argument, but he still felt that people of low birth would not be able to grasp the subtle essence of the Buddha's teaching. They were suited only for menial jobs. Raising them to the status of disciples of the Sangha was not a wise step.

"That *bhikkhu* who was sitting out there when I came in – how well he had understood your teachings, Lord! Now consider someone who is born into a low caste and is unlettered, like Sunita – how can he ever hope to reach such an understanding? Including such people into the Sangha will harm the cause of Dhamma."

Then the Buddha informed him that the young monk who had held him rapt in attention was none other than the night soil carrier, Sunita! The King was dumbfounded and realised at once that all beings carry within themselves infinite possibilities of development. He begged the Buddha's pardon for not having understood his teachings in their entirety.

"I must have accumulated a lot of good Karma, to have the privilege of sitting in the presence of such a great Master," he said.

THE FINAL MONTHS

The Buddha had grown old now, his firm muscular body growing fragile as the years passed. For 45 years the Master had travelled and preached his Doctrine of Liberation and Enlightenment. His voice carried clear and far as before, his eyes gazed with compassion on all beings, just as before.

But many of our companions on the Way were no more with us. Bhikkhunis Gotami and Yashodhara had passed away. So had my dear Rahula, at the age of 51. He served the Sangha well, spreading the message of the Buddha, without ever letting his status as the son of the Master influence his conduct. Rahula remained soft spoken and silent, ever in awe of his father, his devotion shining through his eyes for the world to see.

Moggallana too passed away. His was a horrible death. He had been outspoken and made many enemies as a result. One day, when he emerged from his hut with his two attendants, they were ambushed. They were beaten mercilessly with sticks and stones. Moggallana was in excruciating pain, bleeding profusely, all his bones broken. Unable to bear the pain, he passed into Nirvana. Sariputta grieved Moggallana's death, for they had been like twins in the service of the Buddha.

Where have they all gone, I wondered? Are they all together in some distant plane? The thought was chased out of my mind by the Master's stern voice:

"Do not waste your time on idle speculation, Ananda!"

The Buddha had always discouraged debate and speculation on metaphysics. It is not essential to realising the Way, he said. Bhikkhu Malunkyaputta had persisted though, even threatening to leave the Sangha if the Master did not answer whether the Universe is finite or infinite! And the Master had given a spirited reply:

"Malunkyaputta, you are like a man shot with a poisoned arrow, who refuses to let the physician attend to him! Instead, he wants to know whether the arrow tip is made of wood or metal, which direction it was shot from, what is the nature of poison used, what is the caste of the man who shot it! Such a man will die before the arrow can be removed!

Malunkyaputta, regardless of the finite or infinite nature of the universe, human suffering exists and cannot be denied. My teachings explain the causes of suffering and the Way that leads to their cessation. Following the practice permits you to attain Liberation from the shackles of ignorance, Malunkyaputta. I refuse to comment on anything that is not material to the Path of Liberation!"

My reverie was broken by the sound of a galloping horse approaching in my direction. It was the novice Cunda, Sariputta's attendant. He had been with Sariputta to Nala, where Sariputta's old mother was ailing. Cunda said

Sariputta's mother had passed away. After performing her last rites, Sariputta had gone into his room, sat in the lotus position and passed into Nirvana himself. Blinking back his tears, Cunda handed me a parcel of robes, begging bowl and an urn of ashes.

I could not bear this news. Clutching the parcel, I ran to find the Master. Venerable Sariputta had been his greatest disciple. He had worked his entire life to further the cause of the Dhamma. His sermons on the Great Way had inspired hundreds of young men and women to join the Sangha. He was the one who organised the Sangha as it grew, making sure that all novice monks had appropriate guidance.

The Master heard the news and sat silently for a while. Then he said,

"Why do you grieve so, Ananda? I have explained before, what is born must die. All phenomena are transient, so it is with Sariputta! He served the Dhamma well. His was a life dedicated to attaining and spreading the message of the Great Liberation. He lives on in the Dhamma, Ananda. In all the young men and women who practice the Way, he lives on!"

"But Master, without Moggallana and Sariputta, who will guide the young practitioners now?"

"Many more such beings will take birth and lead the way, Ananda. The Sangha already has many sincere and devoted practitioners. They will carry the message of the Dhamma forward, fear-not!" he comforted me.

A few weeks later, we were in the land of the Licchavis. The Buddha called me aside.

"I have decided Ananda. In three months I will leave this body," he announced.

The ground shook beneath my feet. I implored him not to, I begged him not to abandon his disciples. "I have not yet attained the Great Awakening, O Lord!" I beseeched him.

"What more can I teach you, Ananda? Have I not taught you all I know? Is there anything I have kept secret and hidden from the Sangha? The seeds of Enlightenment are within you. Become your own guide and cling to the Dhamma as the only refuge. Be ever vigilant and you will attain the final deliverance. How long can I live in this body of mine?" he asked softly.

The Buddha asked all the *bhikkhus* and *bhikkhunis* in that region to assemble in Kutagarashala, the monastery that the Licchavi nobles had built. He announced to them that in three months he would pass away and exhorted them to steadfastly practise, realise and transmit the Teachings.

As we went for alms into the city of Vesali the next day, he said this would be the last time he would see the city. My heart grew heavier, but I did not speak.

We travelled northwards, instructing *bhikkhus* in many towns along the way to Pava. They gathered in large numbers to receive his direct teaching for the last time. He reminded them not to accept a teaching, merely because someone said that they had received it directly from the Buddha.

"If anyone gives a discourse on the Teaching, think about it before embracing it. Question it, verify for yourself whether it is in accord with the *sutras* and precepts of our Order. Only then should you embrace it."

At Pava, the blacksmith's son Cunda invited us for a meal offering. The Buddha realised that the mushrooms were spoiled and asked him not to serve them to anyone else. That night he was severely ill with stomach cramps. Next morning, although he was weak with exhaustion, we made our way to the Sal forest outside Kusinara, the city of the Mallas.

Looking at the Sal trees in full bloom, he said, "Let us rest here awhile."

I placed his folded robe on the ground, so he could rest between two Sal trees, his head facing the north. I could not bear to see his condition any longer and I walked away to hide my tears. He sent Aniruddha to get me.

"Don't weep so, Ananda!" he said softly. "There must be dissolution for there to be springing forth! We must part, be torn away from our loved ones, for only after separation can there be coming together.

You have been the most devoted attendant I have had, caring for my smallest need as if it were the most important task to be performed. I am grateful for your care, Ananda, it provided me great comfort! You have acquired immense merit with your service. Now strive hard to break free from the cycle of birth and death. That is the final service you can render me." Then he turned to the rest of the *bhikkhus* accompanying us and said:

"Ananda has been a wise and discreet attendant. He was always pleasant in his manner and knew when to allow visitors to see me. While they waited for me, he spoke to them words of wisdom that filled them with happiness and made them yearn to hear more. He has been a good disciple and a humble servant of the Master."

He then asked me to summon the nobles of Kusinara, telling them that the Buddha would pass into Nirvana that night. The Mallas hurried over to the Sal forest. The people of Kusinara wailed and wept, for the Master was passing away from their midst far too soon.

Among the crowds there was an ascetic, Subhadda, who asked to meet the Buddha, for he had some questions about his teachings.

"Not now, kind sir," I said to him. "The Master is ill and very weak. Please let him rest!"

The ascetic was persistent but I stood firm in my resolve. This was not the time to disturb the Buddha. But he heard our voices and asked for Subhadda to be brought before him.

"Monk Gautama, there have been many famous teachers of other schools. Have they discovered the Truth or have they not?" Subhadda asked.

"It does not matter whether they attained the Truth or not,
Subhadda!" the Buddha replied. "You listen to me well now.
If there is any doctrine or discipline wherein you find the
Noble Eightfold Path, there you will find practitioners who
have discovered the Truth. In any doctrine or discipline which
does not contain the Noble Eightfold Path, none of the
practitioners will realise the Truth."

Then he explained to Subhadda the Noble Eightfold Path,
the guiding light shining bright even in the final moments.
The ascetic sought refuge in the Master's teaching. He was
the last disciple to be ordained by the Buddha.

Then the Buddha spoke to the disciples around him:

"*Bhikkhus*, if you have any doubts, any questions about the
Buddha, the Dhamma, the Sangha or the Path and what is
right conduct, seek your answers now. Do not regret later
that you did not resolve your doubts while your Teacher was
still in your midst."

The *bhikkhus* were silent. Three times he asked thus and
no one had any questions.

"Master, I believe there is none among us who has any doubts
regarding the Buddha, the Dhamma, the Sangha, or the Path
and the way of right conduct!" I exclaimed.

"You say that from faith and belief in the community, Ananda.
As for me, I *know* that there is not a single *bhikkhu* here
who will slip back. All will attain the final deliverance!"

He then looked at each one of us with deep compassion and offered his final advice:

"All material beings ultimately decay. Practise with diligence."

Laying himself down quietly, he passed into Nirvana.

And the Sal blossoms drifted down gently through the night.

EPILOGUE

Venerable Mahakassapa called a meeting in Rajagaha of all
the *bhikkhus* and a group of 500 was selected to agree upon
the content of the Buddha's teachings. I was selected too, as
I had been present on most occasions, having been his
attendant. I could recall each of the Buddha's discourses in
great detail.

I was despondent at the Buddha's death, however. For this, I
received a stern admonishment from Mahakassapa.

"Ananda, though you have been the Buddha's attendant and
companion for many years, I am inclined not to let you even
enter the Dhamma Hall! You have not yet attained the Great
Awakening!"

I took that to heart. For three days I sat in my hut, meditating
upon the Dhamma. At the end of the third day I was tired
and decided to lie down for a while. As my back touched the
ground, I attained the Great Awakening.

It was a fine morning as I set off for walking meditation.

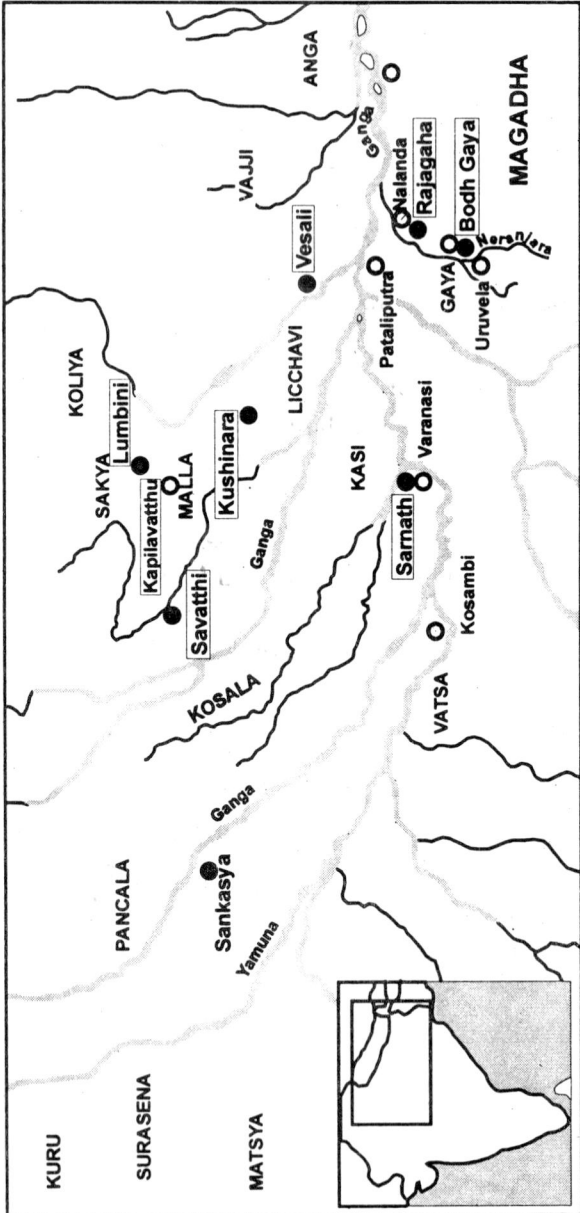

THE BUDDHA TRAIL

It is possible to visit the places mentioned in this book. Some are known by new names now and many have temples, stupas or pillars with edicts to mark the sacred site. Given below is a listing of some of the places that can be toured:

Lumbini (Nepal): The Buddha's birthplace has a temple complex that houses the tank where Queen Mahamaya had her bath before delivery. King Ashoka erected a pillar, Rummendei pillar, to mark the place.

Kapilavatthu, now known as Kapilavastu. The Buddha spent the first 30 years of his life here. Ruins of the palace can still be seen.

Uruvela, on the banks of the river Neranjara, where the Buddha attained enlightenment, is now known as Bodh Gaya. The magnificent Mahabodhi temple has seven sacred sites within its precincts. Prominent among these is the Bodhi tree, not the original, but its descendant, and the *vajrasana*, the Diamond Throne, a red sandstone slab marking the spot of the Buddha's meditation. Inside the temple is a beautiful image of the Buddha in the 'Bhumisparsha' (touching the Earth) mudra.

The Deer Park, at Isipatana (Skt:Rishipattana) where the Buddha met his five ascetic companions is now known as

Sarnath. Sarnath housed a monastery for 1500 years. In the third century BC King Ashoka erected a column 15.24m in height with four lions as its capital. This was adopted as the emblem of the modern Indian republic. Of the two great stupas that marked this site only the Dhamekha remains. It marks the sacred place where the Buddha gave his first sermon.

Rajagaha, the capital of the erstwhile Magadha kingdom, is now known as Rajgir. There one can visit the Gijjhakuta (Skt:Griddhakuta) hill, where the Buddha spent many long days in meditation and where Devadatta had tried to kill him by sending a boulder hurtling down the slope. At Rajgir is the Venuvana monastery, the Bamboo Grove donated by King Bimbisara.

Vesali, now known as Vaishali: It was here that women were first ordained into the Sangha. Amvara, the neighbouring village, is the site of Ambapali's mango grove dwelling. She gifted it to the Sangha and joined the order herself. It was in Vaishali that the Buddha declared the imminent Mahaparinirvana. King Ashoka has built a stupa to mark the spot.

Savatthi is now Sravasti. This was the Buddha's monsoon retreat for 25 years. Jetavana vihara, built by Sudatta, contains the ruins of Anandakuti and Gandhakuti, where Buddha stayed and expounded the Dhamma and formulated some of the Rules of monastic discipline. The Angulimala incident also happened in Sravasti

Kushinara, (now Kushinagar) was the place where the Buddha lay down between two Sal trees and passed into

Mahaparinirvana. The Mahaparinirvana temple enshrines a statue in that posture. Close to the temple is Mathakuar shrine, where he delivered his last sermon.

GLOSSARY

Ashoka: *Saraca indica* ; an evergreen tree with deep green foliage and orange-yellow flowers, which turn red. Sanskrit: *shoka* – sorrow; Ashoka – that which gives no grief.

bhikkhus: monks of the Buddhist order. Sanskrit: *bhikshus*; from *bhiksha* – alms. The monks begged for the one meal that they ate in the day and depended on the laity for donations of robes and medicines.

Dhamma: the Doctrine of the Buddha; Sanskrit: *dharma*; also refers to the law, the social or moral order.

gatha: a four-line verse that encapsulates the various aspects of the Doctrine.

Jambu: *Syzigium jambos*; the Rose Apple tree, offers cool shade with its leathery leaves and great span of branches; has pale yellow fruits with a pink blush; the flesh is crisp and sweet with the flavour of roses.

Karma: literally, deeds. The theory that good or bad actions from the past determine an individual's present life. A person accumulates Karma that will bear fruit in the future.

Mandara: *Erythrina indica*; the Indian coral, a tree with spiny, bright red flowers. According to Buddhist legends, the heavens showered Mandara blossoms on the newborn Prince Siddhartha.

Nirvana: a state when the mind is freed from all defilements and passions.

Peepal: *Ficus religiosa*; a tree with heart shaped leaves. The Buddha attained enlightenment under this tree and it is therefore referred to as the Bodhi tree in Buddhist literature.

Sal: *Shorea robusta*; a tree that grows wild in north, east and central India; has whitish flowers; its wood is one of the three naturally lasting timbers of the Asian continent, the other two being teak and deodar.

Sangha: the community of monks belonging to the order founded by the Buddha.

sindoor: a bright red powder with which women mark a round spot in the center of their forehead or apply in the parting of their hair – as a sign of marital felicity.

sutras: short prose passages that enabled the monks to memorise the Doctrine.

sutradhar: one who holds the threads of the narrative.

Vesakha: the second month of the Hindu calendar, corresponding with April-May. Sanskrit: Vaisakha.

vihara: a monastery.